I0842688

TACKLING MEDICARE

A SIMPLE GUIDE TO UNDERSTANDING
What You Need To Know About Medicare

David Kurtz

President of Senior Benefit Services, Inc.

The **Author**

HELLO THERE! I'M DAVID KURTZ

Right now I would guess that you are really not all that interested in me, but rather how Senior Benefit Services, Inc and its advisors can help you transition into being on Medicare. That is exactly how your mindset should be. The reality is that Medicare is overwhelming!

Fortunately for you, I have been personally licensed and specializing in the Medicare market for well over 30 years. In fact, when I was 14 years old, my father made me start helping him do Medicare claim filing for his clients (which didn't impress the teenage girls back then either). Back in those days, there was very little if any Medicare claims crossover (where Medicare would send the claim on to the insurance company for the provider to be paid) so this was either done by the insured or their agent. Our goal is to help you understand the basics of

Medicare so that you are not completely overwhelmed as you approach age 65.

I pride myself on having what I would consider not only the most knowledgeable advisors working for our company, but ones who always put our client's first!

If trying to understand everything about Medicare wasn't complicated enough, you have to sort thru all of the 'information' (or should I say junk mail) that will be hitting your mailbox very soon. By the end of this book, you should feel very comfortable with throwing most of that crap right in the garbage.

Copyright © 2026 by David Kurtz, Senior Benefit Services, Inc.

All rights reserved. Except as permitted under the U.S. Copyright Act of 1976, no part of this publication may be reproduced, distributed, or transmitted in any form without the prior permission of the copyright owner.

ISBN: 979-8-9889580-1-7

Introduction

Let's just put this out there in the open…the Medicare program is very overwhelming! The federal government wants you to be able to simply read their publication Medicare & You (which you get when you are turning 65) and select everything that you are going to need to be properly insured. Really?? Between all the mail you get from insurance companies wanting you to enroll in one of their plans to the crazy (and many times misleading) TV commercials that talk about getting benefits that seem too good to be true, how could anyone make this important of a decision on their own.

My goal is to make Medicare easy for you to understand. Of course, I do not recommend trying to navigate Medicare and all the options on your own. I highly recommend you work with an insurance professional who has expertise in dealing with Medicare-specific plans. Keep in mind that there is no such thing as a one plan fits all scenario. Insurance agents who simply push a product are what I refer to as commission hunters. They want to sell you a plan as quick as possible so they can move onto the next prospect. A specialist will take the time to see what your personal needs are and then recommend several different options.

Over the decades, myself and our advisors have helped tens of thousands of clients navigate the Medicare maze and obtain coverage that works best for them. I personally got my start in the insurance business at age 14 by helping my father file his client's claims with the insurance company. Now, I am well into being licensed for over 30 years and have remained focused on the ever-changing world of Medicare.

In this book, I will walk you through the main areas of Medicare and how to:

- Enroll on time to avoid any penalties
- Help you understand the two different paths you can take with Medicare
- Why you should review your plan each year with your agent
- Enroll in the prescription plan best for you. Also see why you need a prescription drug plan even if you don't currently take any prescriptions
- Avoid being sold a plan that does not work for you

Table of Contents

CHAPTER 1:
A Short History Lesson on Medicare

A Short History Lesson on Medicare

The Medicare program was established in 1965 as a part of the Social Security Act Amendments. President Lyndon B. Johnson signed the bill, which provided federal health insurance coverage for Americans ages 65 and older who had paid into Social Security. Traditional Medicare is comprised of Parts A & B. Prior to the creation of Medicare, healthcare coverage was scarce for many seniors, and many individuals found themselves unable to afford medical care after retirement. Medicare has since expanded to include people with disabilities and those with End-Stage Renal Disease, providing crucial healthcare services to millions of Americans.

Medicare Part C, also known as Medicare Advantage, was first created as a part of the Balanced Budget Act of 1997. Sorry to say, this initial attempt at Part C was a bit of a failure and most of these plans disappeared within a couple of years. At the same time Medicare Part D was created, Part C was revitalized thru government funded subsidies to private insurance companies.

Medicare Advantage offers all the coverage provided by Medicare Parts A and B through private insurance companies that are approved by Medicare. The creation of Medicare Advantage was intended to increase the number of coverage options available to seniors by allowing private companies to provide healthcare services. Medicare Advantage plans typically offer additional benefits beyond traditional Medicare, such as prescription drug coverage, vision, and hearing coverage. Seniors can enroll in Medicare Advantage plans during specific enrollment periods and must continue to pay their monthly Part B premium. Even though an enrollee will continue to pay their

Part B premium, all medical claims must be filed directly to the plan and not to Medicare itself.

Medicare Part D was created in 2003 as part of the Medicare Prescription Drug, Improvement, and Modernization Act. This program was established to help seniors pay for prescription drug costs. Before the implementation of Part D, Medicare did not provide coverage for prescription drugs, leaving many older Americans struggling to pay for their medications. Before 2003 there were only 3 standardized Medicare Supplement plans that provided any form of prescription drug coverage. These plans were very expensive and after the introduction of Medicare Part D, these plans were phased out. Part D provides coverage for generic and brand-name prescription drugs and is administered by private insurance companies that are approved by Medicare. Seniors can enroll in a Part D plan to help reduce their out-of-pocket costs for prescription medications. It is important to understand that you cannot have both a Medicare Advantage plan and a stand-alone Part D prescription drug plan.

IMPORTANT: A recent change that took place in 2018 was the removal of a Medicare beneficiary's social security number and replaced it with a Medicare Beneficiary Identifier (MBI) in an effort to protect against identity theft.

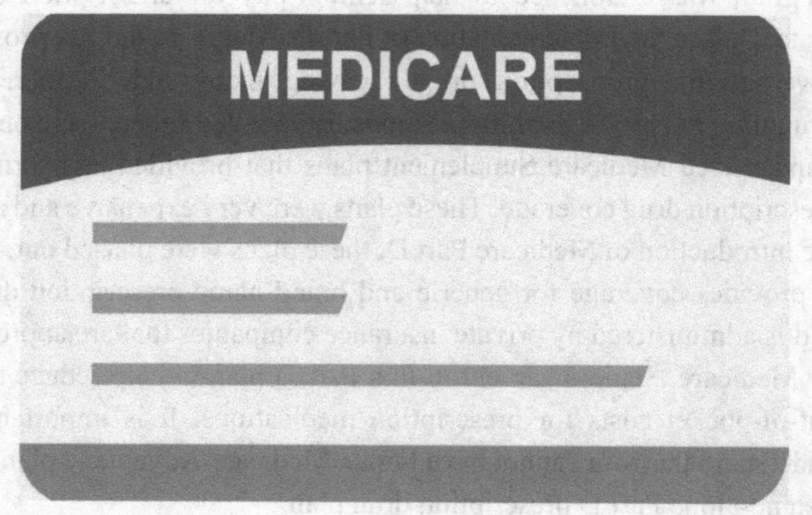

CHAPTER 2:
Understanding the Basics
of Medicare Parts

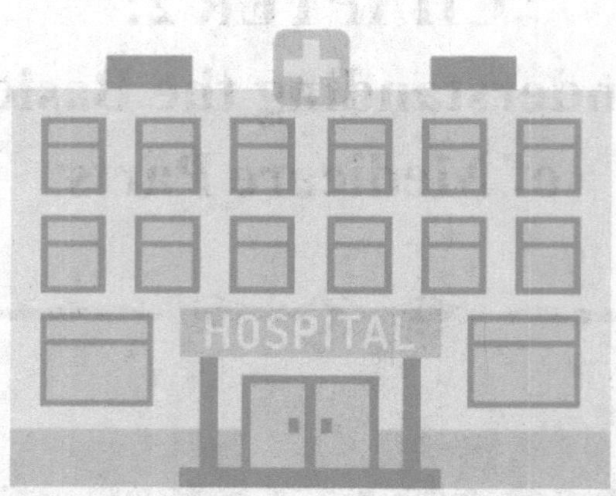

Medicare Part A

Medicare Part A is hospital insurance designed to cover inpatient hospital care, hospice care, some home health care, and nursing facility care. Part A has no monthly premium charges (if you or your spouse worked enough quarters). The reality is that most older Americans qualify for premium free Part A. To apply for Medicare Part A, individuals must have either paid into Social Security or worked for the government for a specific period.

Medicare Part B

Medicare Part B, on the other hand, is medical insurance that covers outpatient services like doctor visits, medical equipment, and preventive care services. It does not cover long-term care and does not include dental, vision, or hearing coverage. Medicare Part B requires a monthly premium, and fees vary depending on income level. It is important to note that the standard monthly Part B premium you pay only covers about 25% of the actual costs and that the government is subsidizing the other 75%.

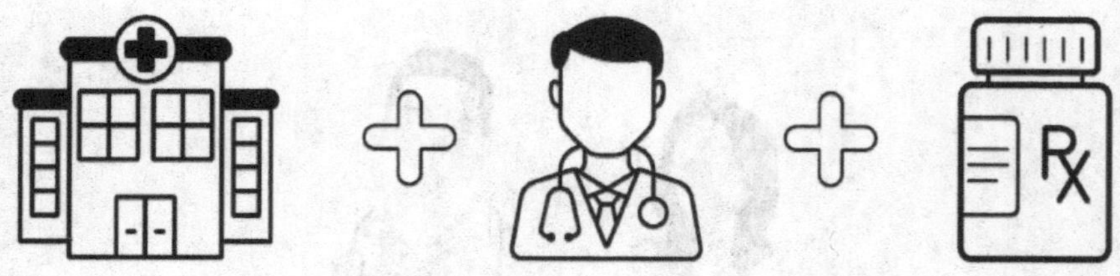

Medicare Part C

Medicare Part C, also known as Medicare Advantage, provides all the coverage offered by Parts A and B through private insurance companies approved by the government. Medicare Advantage plans typically offer additional benefits beyond traditional Medicare, such as prescription drug coverage, vision, and hearing coverage. Individuals enrolled in Medicare Advantage pay a separate monthly premium to cover the additional benefits. It is important to remember that just because a Medicare Advantage plan has to provide the same benefits as traditional Medicare, it can require you to get prior authorization or have you try a different treatment first.

Medicare Part D

Medicare Part D is prescription drug coverage, and it is available for purchase as a standalone policy or can be part of a Medicare Advantage plan (commonly referred to as an MAPD). This coverage assists in covering the cost of prescription drugs and comes with a monthly premium, which varies depending on the plan and the individual's income level.

Chapter Wrap-Up

In conclusion, understanding the different parts of Medicare is necessary to take advantage of all available healthcare benefits. Medicare Parts A and B form the traditional Medicare program, while Medicare Part C or Medicare Advantage and Part D offer additional coverage options. Seniors must consider their healthcare needs, including prescription medications, vision, and hearing in choosing an appropriate Medicare plan.

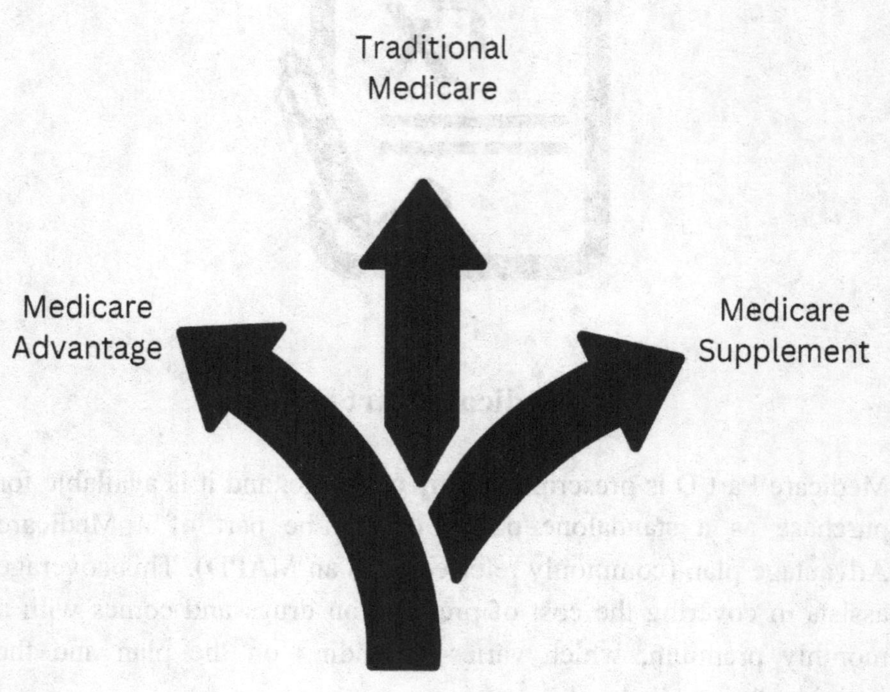

CHAPTER 3:
Understanding Medicare
Part A

Understanding Part A

As we mentioned before, Medicare Part A is designed to help cover the costs of medical care and treatment in an inpatient facility such as a hospital, skilled nursing facility, or rehabilitation center. Many folks are confused by the benefits of a skilled nursing facility and interpret that to mean they have long term care coverage. This is not the case!

Part A also covers certain home health care services and Hospice care for those facing terminal illness. It includes the costs associated with hospitalization, such as room and board, nursing services, surgical and ancillary services. Medicare Part A also covers some preventative care like flu shots and certain screenings.

In most situations, Americans who have had a 10-year history of taxable employment, or those married to someone with the same work history, will be eligible to receive Part A coverage free of charge. This is true regardless of whether they are still working or are retired. The only exceptions are if an individual has not paid enough in Medicare taxes over the years or is a member of the Railroad Retirement Board. In those cases, there may be a cost to receive Part A coverage. It's important to note that without Part A coverage, an individual would not be eligible for any of the other parts of Medicare. If you nor your spouse worked enough quarters, then the cost for Part A of Medicare will be quite expensive to obtain (see Figure 1).

Monthly Medicare Part A Premium 2026

40 work quarters = $0.00
30 work quarters = $311.00
<30 work quarters = $565.00

https://www.cms.gov/newsroom/fact-sheets/2026-medicare-parts-b-premiums-deductibles

Since Part A has been paid for with Medicare taxes taken out of your pay each period, it is highly recommended that everyone enrolls in it. Note that Health Savings Account (HSA) holders are an exception to this rule. The coverage will be effective on the first day of the month which coincides with the birth month. This is consistent for all Medicare-related coverages.

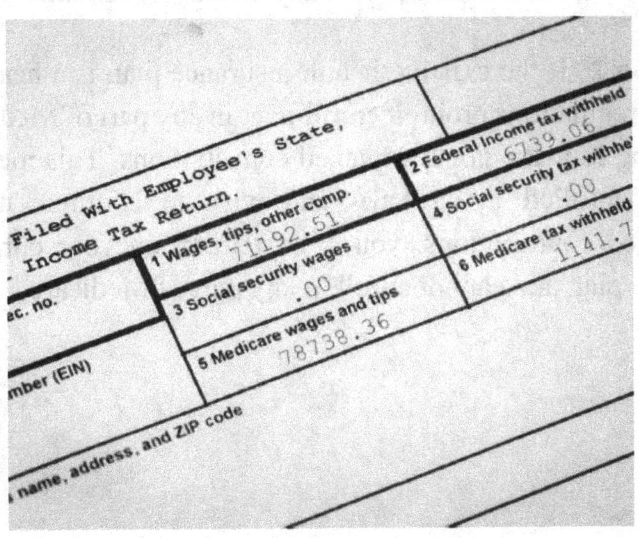

Generally, individuals who are nearing the age of 65 may enroll in Medicare up to three months before their birthday month begins. This means that coverage would kick off on the first day of their birth month. As Part A is usually free of charge, it is wise to enroll as early as possible to take advantage of this benefit.

If you plan to enroll in Medicare Part A after your birth month, you have a three-month period available to do so. However, this could mean going without coverage for some time. It is best to check with the Social Security Administration prior to enrolling in Part A, especially if you are transitioning from an employer's group insurance plan. This will ensure that your Medicare coverage starts when your other plan ends.

Exception To The Rule: If the individual's actual date of birth falls on the first day of any month, their eligibility for coverage will begin the month before. As a result, Medicare coverage for the individual will become effective on the first day of the prior month.

Exception 2: If the existing health insurance plan is a health savings account, regulations prohibit enrollment in any part of Medicare while continuing to make tax advantaged contributions. This means that, if you are enrolled in an HSA and wish to continue making tax advantaged contributions, you must remain on your current health insurance plan and cannot enroll in any part of Medicare.

It is important to note that if a person is already enrolled in Medicare and has an existing HSA, contributions can no longer be made to their HSA, but the funds still remain.1 The individual must use the funds from the HSA for qualified medical expenses or else they may be subject to taxes and penalties. Furthermore, if an individual enrolls in Medicare and has an existing HSA, they cannot make any new contributions to the account. However, they are still able to use the funds from their HSA for qualified medical expenses.

Example: Jane is turning 65 and enrolls in Parts A & B and decides that a Medicare Supplement Plan G is the right choice for her needs. When Jane retired from her job, she had $10,000 in her HSA plan. While Jane can no longer contribute to her HSA plan, she does not lose the funds that are already saved in there. This means that Jane can access those funds to pay for such things as co-pays on her prescription drug refills, vision and hearing expenses, and quite a large number of over-the-counter items.

CHAPTER 4:
Understanding Medicare
Part B

UNDERSTANDING PART B

Medicare Part B is designed to cover medically necessary and preventive services, including doctor visits, laboratory tests, medical equipment, and some outpatient services. One of the biggest areas of confusion is when a doctor sees a patient in the hospital. Most would think that those charges would be covered under Part A, but in actuality the doctor must still bill their charges under Part B of Medicare.

ELIGIBILITY FOR MEDICARE PART B

Individuals who have qualified for Medicare Part A are automatically eligible to enroll in Medicare Part B. Part B coverage is available to all Americans aged 65 and older, as well as some younger individuals with certain disabilities or end-stage renal disease. There are specific enrollment periods for Medicare Part B, and it's crucial to enroll during an appropriate time to avoid penalties. While enrolling in Part B is not mandatory, you will not be able to enroll in a Medicare Supplement or Medicare Advantage plan if you are not enrolled in Part B. Those who do not enroll in Part B will be responsible for 100% of the costs for any services rendered under this part of Medicare. This means that if you have a surgery and that doctor charges $30,000 for their part, then you will be liable to pay the full $30,000 rather than just 20% ($6,000 left over after Medicare would have paid its 80% of the approved charges).

Important: If you do not enroll in Medicare Part B when you are first eligible and do not qualify to defer enrollment, then you will be subject to a late enrollment penalty. In fact, the 10% extra that you will be subject to pay is not just a one-time penalty, but that is recalculated and paid each year for the remainder of your life. Below you will see an example of how this penalty works.

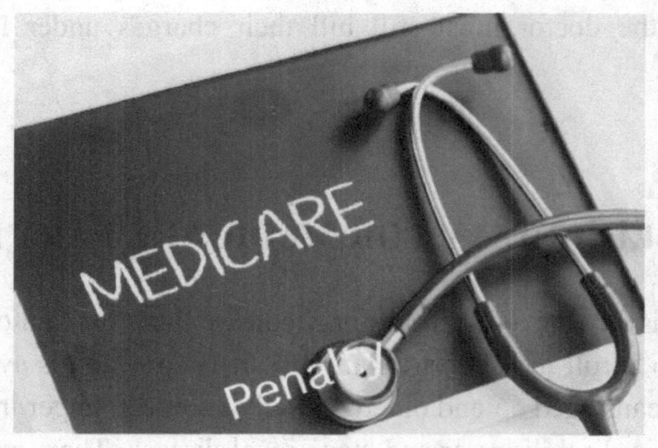

If you waited 3 full years (36 months)) to sign up for Part B and didn't qualify for a Special Enrollment Period (SEP), you will have to pay a 30% penalty for late enrollment in addition to your standard Part B monthly premium. The Part B standard premium for 2026 is $202.90 per month.

Computation: $202.90 (Part B Premium) + $60.87 (30% penalty) = $263.77

$263.77 monthly premium is then rounded to the nearest .10 cents = $263.80

COVERED SERVICES UNDER MEDICARE PART B

Medicare Part B covers a broad range of services that are necessary for maintaining good health and wellness. These services include:

- Medically necessary services: Doctor visits, outpatient surgery, laboratory tests, and diagnostic services are all covered by Medicare Part B. Even surgeons who perform services while you are an inpatient in the hospital must still bill their charges under Part B of Medicare.
- Preventive services: Certain preventive services, such as flu shots, diabetes screenings, and mammograms, are covered under Medicare Part B without any out-of-pocket costs.
- Durable medical equipment: Devices such as wheelchairs, scooters, oxygen equipment, and walkers are covered under Medicare Part B. Home health care:
- Home health care services such as skilled nursing services, occupational therapy, and speech-language pathology services are covered by Medicare Part B.
- Mental health services: Mental health services, including preventive services, counseling, and therapy, are covered under Medicare Part B.

COSTS ASSOCIATED WITH MEDICARE PART B

There are costs associated with Medicare Part B, including monthly premiums, deductibles, and cost-sharing requirements. The premium amount for Medicare Part B changes annually and is typically determined by the individual's income level. See Figure 2

Figure 2

2026 Income-Related Monthly Adjustment Amounts		
2026 Medicare Part B Monthly Premiums		
File Individual Tax Return	File Joint Tax Return	Total Monthly Premium Amount
$109,000 or below	$218,000 or less	$202.90
$109,001 - $137,000	$218,001 - $274,000	$284.10
$137,001 - $171,000	$274,001 - $342,000	$405.80
$171,001 - $ 205,000	$342,001 - $410,000	$527.50
$205,001 - $500,000	$410,001 - $750,000	$649.20
$500,001 and greater	$750,001 and greater	$689.90

The additional premium that higher income earners pay is known as IRMAA. It is important to understand that the additional amount of Part B premiums that a high-income earner will be responsible for is based upon their income tax returns from 2 years ago. This means that your 2026 Part B premiums are based on income from 2024. If you've had a life-changing event that reduced your household income, you can appeal the IRMAA amounts with Social Security by completing the Medicare Income-Related Monthly Adjustment Life Changing Event (SSA-44) form.

Before being able to start an appeal, you must receive the formal notification showing the higher premium from Medicare.2

In addition to monthly premiums, beneficiaries are required to pay an annual deductible before Medicare Part B coverage kicks in. Beneficiaries are also responsible for paying a portion of the cost-sharing requirements for various covered services. These amounts are typically 20% of the Medicare approved amounts.

CHAPTER 5:
Understanding Medicare
Part D

Understanding Medicare Part D

Medicare Part D provides prescription drug coverage to help beneficiaries cover the cost of their medications. This program is funded through monthly premiums paid by beneficiaries and is available to all Medicare beneficiaries.

ELIGIBILITY FOR MEDICARE PART D

To be eligible for Medicare Part D, individuals must be enrolled in Medicare Part A or Part B. Most Medicare Advantage plans that are enrolled in offer prescription drug coverage, but an individual who wants to opt for a standalone Part D plan can do so during their enrollment period.

COVERED MEDICATIONS UNDER PART D

Medicare Part D covers a wide range of prescription drugs, including both brand-name and generic medications. However, there are certain medications, such as weight-loss drugs, over-the-counter drugs, and cosmetic drugs that are not covered.

COSTS ASSOCIATED WITH PART D

Medicare Part D entails monthly premiums, deductibles, and out-of-pocket costs. The monthly premium for Part D varies based on the chosen plan, and it is essential to choose a plan that fits your budget and covers your required medications.

In addition to premiums, there are deductibles for Medicare Part D coverage. After the deductible amount is paid, beneficiaries are responsible for a portion of their medication costs. They are responsible for paying copayments, coinsurance, and the remaining cost-sharing obligation once the deductible has been met. One thing to keep in mind is that some plans do not have a deductible, but their monthly premium may be higher than plans that do have a deductible.

THE COVERAGE GAP IN MEDICARE PART D

Prior to 2025, Medicare Part D beneficiaries would receive coverage for their prescription drugs up to a certain spending limit, then they entered what was known as the "coverage gap" or "donut hole." While in this phase, beneficiaries were required to pay a percentage of their medication costs out-of-pocket until they reached a higher spending threshold. Once that threshold was met, they moved into the catastrophic phase, where they were only responsible for copays.

In 2026, the coverage gap phase is once again eliminated entirely. Instead, Medicare Part D will implement a $2,100 annual out-of-pocket cap on prescription drug costs. After reaching this cap, beneficiaries will no longer pay anything for their covered prescriptions for the remainder of the year.

Like Medicare Part B, Part D may have an extra premium based on your income from the past two years.3

2026 Income-Related Monthly Adjustment Amounts

2026 Medicare Part D Monthly Premiums		
File Individual Tax Return	File Joint Tax Return	Plan D Premium + Income Adjustment
$109,000 or below	$218,000 or less	Part D Plan Premium
$109,001 - $137,000	$218,001 - $274,000	+$14.50
$137,001 - $171,000	$274,001 - $342,000	+$37.50
$171,001 - $ 205,000	$342,001 - $410,000	+$60.40
$205,001 - $500,000	$410,001 - $750,000	+$83.30
$500,001 and greater	$750,001 and greater	$91.00

CHAPTER 6:
Understanding Medicare
Part C

Understanding Medicare Part C

Medicare Part C, also known as Medicare Advantage, is an alternative way for individuals to receive their Medicare benefits. Medicare Advantage plans are offered through private insurance companies and are required to provide the same coverage options as Medicare Parts A and B. In addition, Medicare Advantage plans may offer additional benefits such as vision, hearing, and prescription drug coverage.

ELIGIBILITY FOR MEDICARE PART C

To be eligible for Medicare Part C, an individual must have Medicare Parts A and B and reside in the plan's service area. Most Medicare Advantage plans are offered to individuals who are 65 years of age or older, but individuals with certain disabilities or end-stage renal disease (ESRD) may also qualify.

COVERED SERVICES UNDER MEDICARE PART C

Medicare Advantage plans offer the same coverage options as Medicare Parts A and B, including medically necessary services, preventive services, and durable medical equipment. In addition, many Medicare Advantage plans provide extra benefits such as vision, hearing, and prescription drug coverage. These benefits are often bundled into the plan's premiums, but some may have separate premiums.

COSTS ASSOCIATED WITH MEDICARE PART C

The costs associated with Medicare Part C can vary depending on the specific plan and benefits offered. Many Medicare Advantage plans have monthly premiums, deductibles, and cost-sharing requirements such as copayments and coinsurance. However, the overall cost may be lower than traditional Medicare because many Medicare Advantage plans include additional benefits. It is important to note that this is comparing Medicare Advantage to having just traditional Medicare Parts A and B. This is not comparing Medicare Advantage plans to having a Medicare Supplement plan to go along with traditional Medicare.

ENROLLMENT PERIODS FOR MEDICARE PART C

Enrollment in Medicare Part C is voluntary and is restricted to certain times of the year. See Figure 4

Figure 4

Initial Election Period

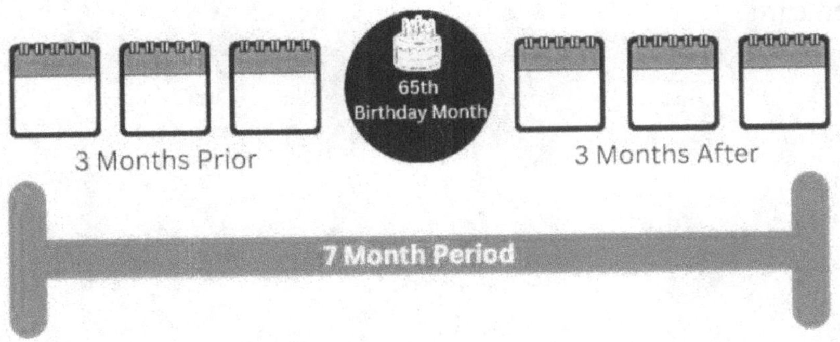

When FIRST eligible for Medicare

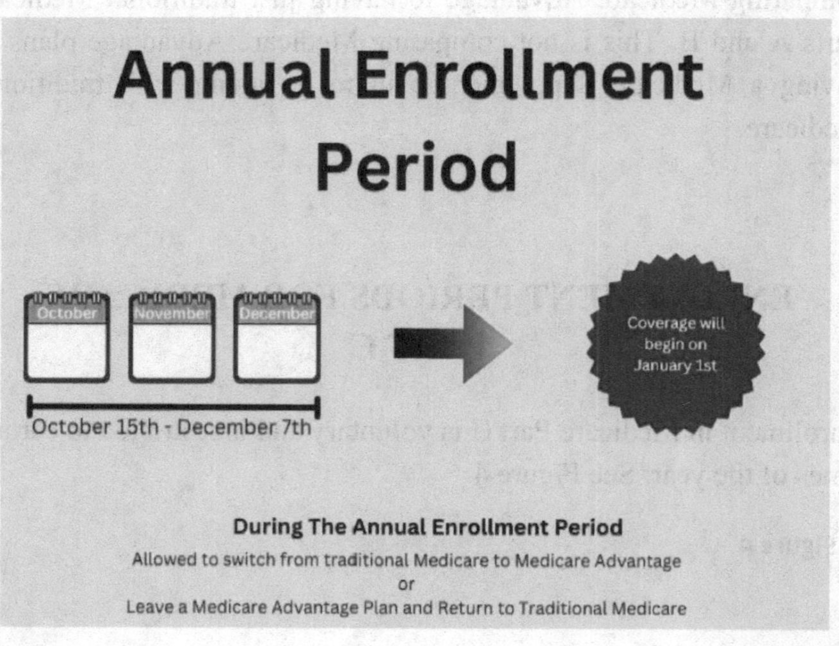

Period runs every year between October 15th - December 7th Allowed to switch from traditional Medicare to Medicare Advantage or Leave a Medicare Advantage Plan and Return to Traditional Medicare

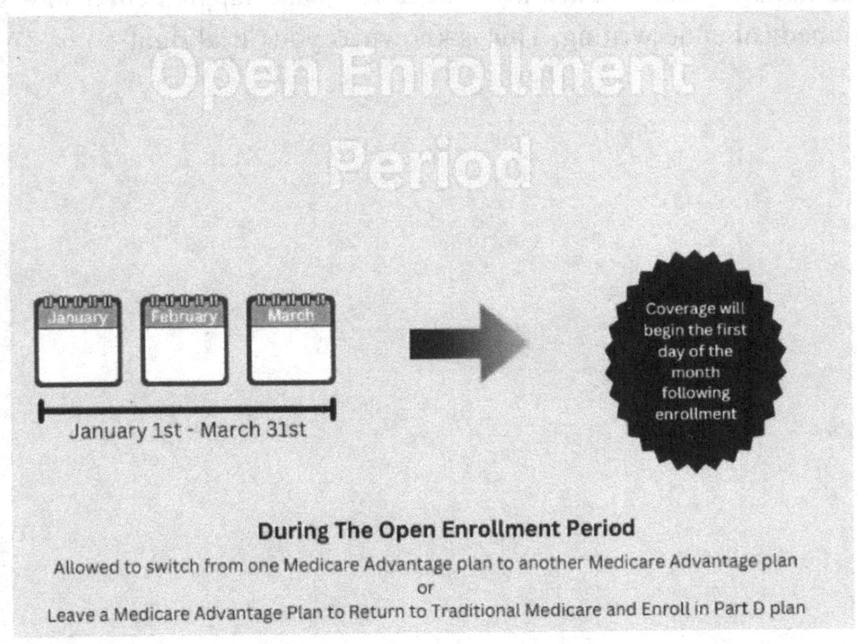

Period runs every year between January 1st - March 31st Allowed to switch from one Medicare Advantage plan to another Medicare Advantage plan or Leave a Medicare Advantage Plan to Return to Traditional Medicare and enroll in a Part D plan

Important Note: Neither the AEP or the OEP for Medicare Advantage and Part D plans provide a guaranteed issue enrollment into a Medicare Supplement plan. If you enroll into a Medicare Advantage plan and then after 1 year decide to return to Traditional Medicare during the AEP or OEP, you will likely need to medically qualify for a Medicare Supplement. If you enrolled directly into a Medicare Advantage plan when first eligible for Medicare and then within the first 11 months decide that it is not for you, then you can return to traditional Medicare and enroll into a Medicare Supplement plan with no medical underwriting. This is known as your 'trial right'.

CHAPTER 7:
How to Apply for Medicare

How to Apply for Medicare

Now that we have gotten the boring basics of Medicare behind us, let's move on to what you need to do if you are enrolling into Medicare for the first time. If you are already on Medicare and have created an online account, please feel free to skip over this chapter.

FIRST THINGS FIRST!

Do you have an online Social Security account? This is an online account that allows you to access all needed information about your social security benefits and will be needed to sign up for Medicare. To create your online my Social Security account take the following steps:

1.   Go to www.ssa.gov/myaccount
2.   Click on Create an Account
3.   You will be sent to the following (next page)

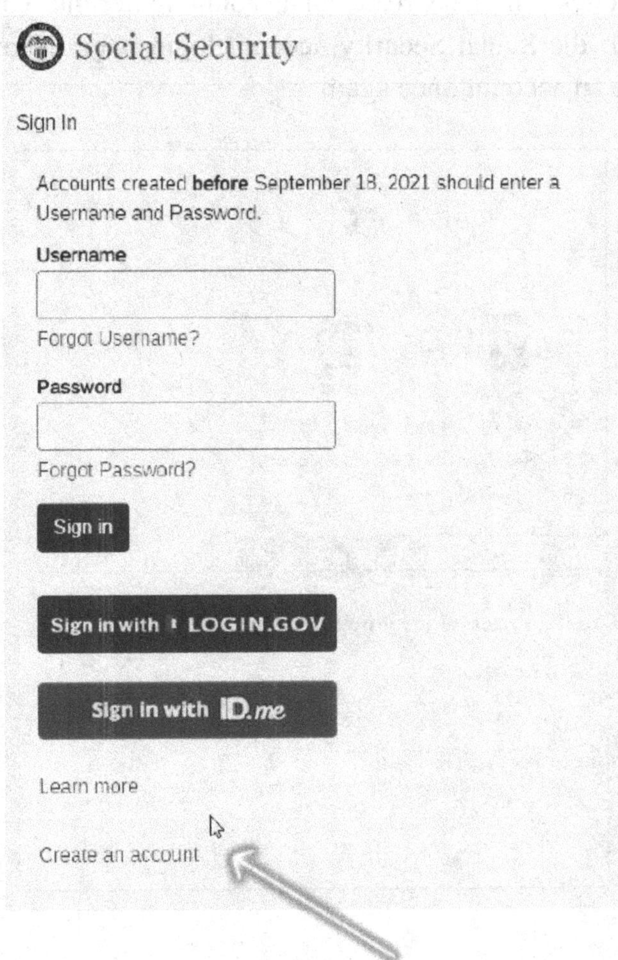

Once you reach this page, you will need to click on the above hyperlink

Once you click on the Create an account hyperlink you will be redirected to the Social Security account login page. Here you will click Create an account once again.

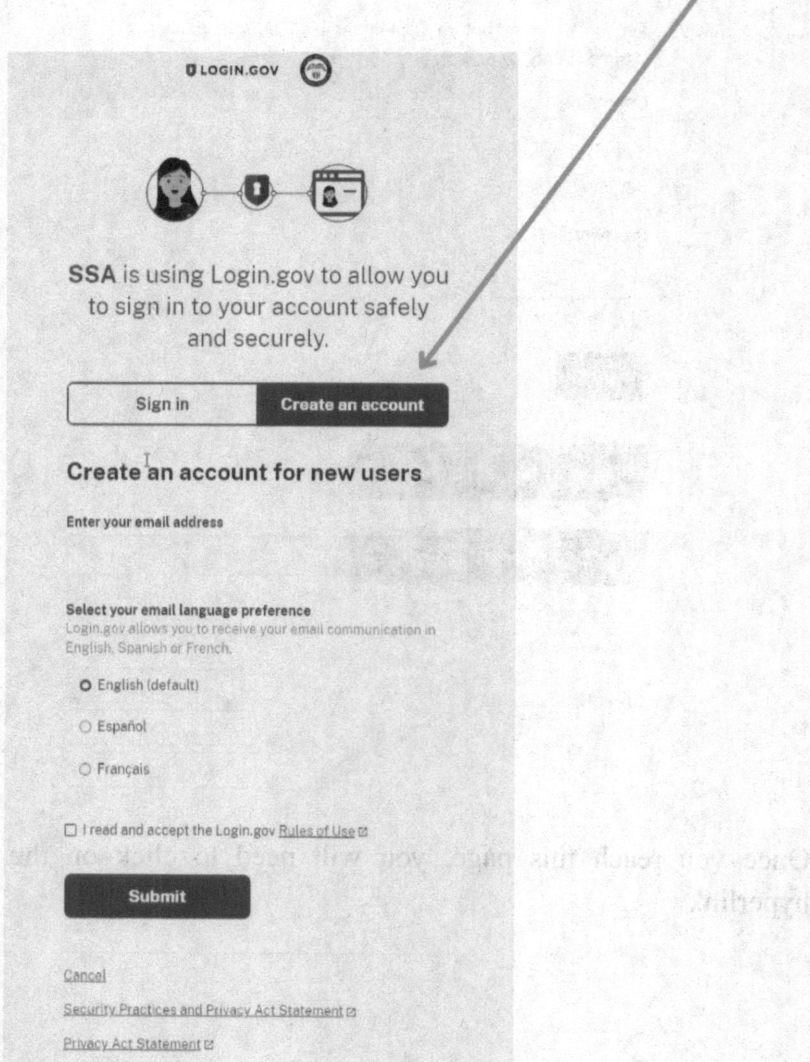

After you have entered all necessary information, you will either receive an email with your account authorization or in some instances it will be mailed to you via USPS.

Before signing up for Medicare we advise you reviewing the eligibility requirements. When turning 65 you are going to be signing up during your 'Initial Enrollment Period'. There is a handy calculator that will allow you to enter your birth date to see when you can enroll and avoid late penalties. To use the calculator go to www.ssa.gov/medicare/plan/when-to-sign-up

The 3 enrollment periods

1. When you're turning 65

This is the "Initial Enrollment Period," and there are no penalties if you sign up during this time.

Enter your birth date to see when you can first enroll:

Select month	Select day	Select year

The 3 enrollment periods

1. When you're turning 65

This is the "Initial Enrollment Period," and there are no penalties if you sign up during this time.

Enter your birth date to see when you can first enroll:

December	16	1961

Enroll between September 1, 2026 and March 31, 2027

If you sign up from September 1, 2026 - November 30, 2026, your coverage will begin December 1, 2026. If you sign up from December 1, 2026 - March 31, 2027, your coverage will begin the first of the month after you sign up.

This individual can enroll between September 1, 2026, and March 31, 2027, without having a late enrollment penalty. The optimal enrollment timeline is September 1, 2026 - November 30, 2026, so that coverage is effective December 1, 2026

When you know that you are eligible to sign up for Medicare and when you should enroll, the next step is to sign into your *my Social Security* account and then start the Medicare enrollment process or you can visit www.ssa.gov/medicare/signup

Before signing up you will need to be able to provide the following:

- Basic information about yourself including (Social Security number, the city, state, and country you were born in)
- Health insurance information (start & end dates for any current group health plans and start and end dates for any group health plans after age 65 if applicable)

Once you have all the necessary information, click on the Apply online button

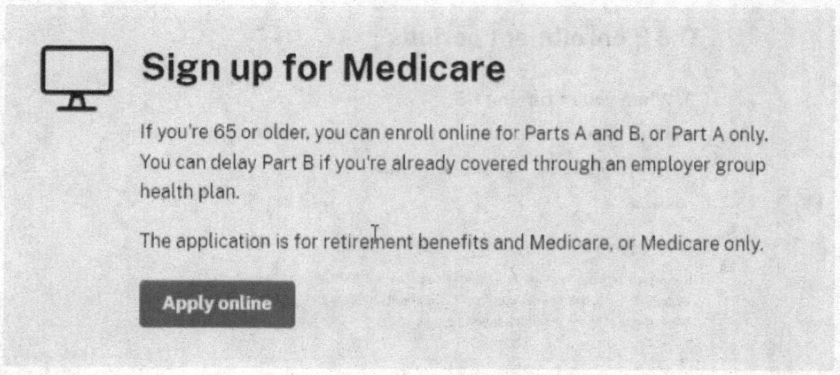

You will then be directed to the Terms of Service page where you click on the box showing you understand and agree to the statements before you can proceed.

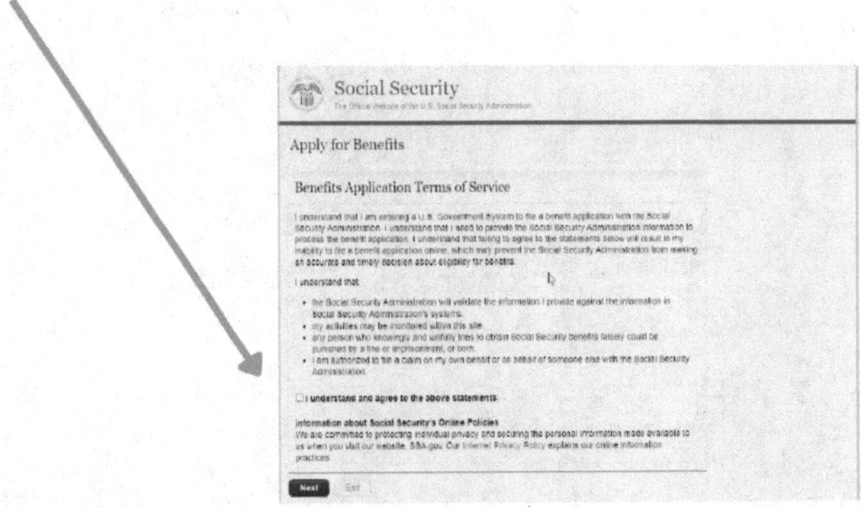

After clicking the box click the Next button

With everything you have done so far, you might be tempted to simply click on the Start a New Application button in the Apply & Complete section. Before doing this, you might find it helpful to click on the Video Introduction which is only 1 minute long.

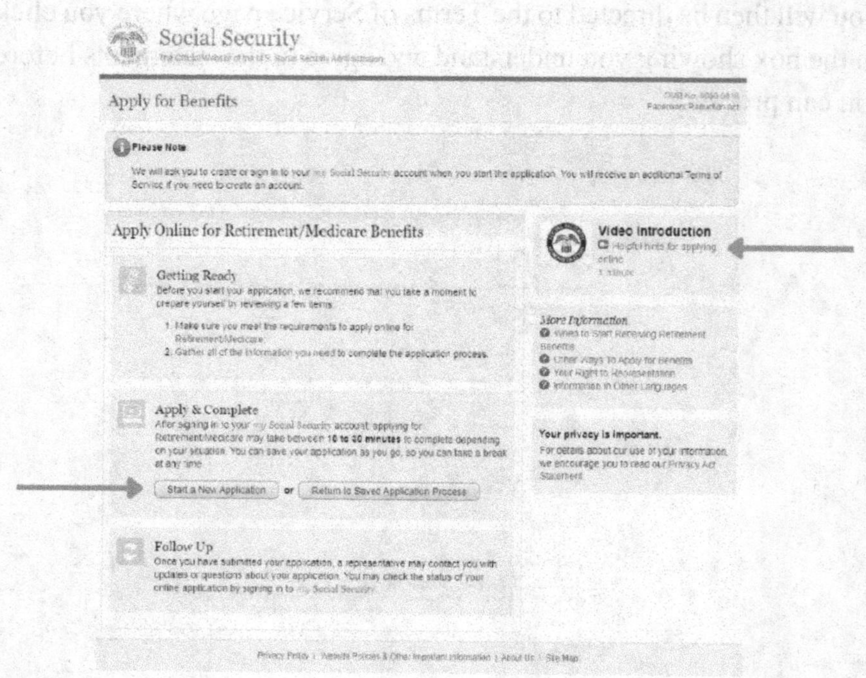

Once you do start your application process you will be prompted to choose that you are applying for yourself. Once you make that selection, it will ask you if you have a my Social Security account. Since we have already done a walk thru on how to set up a my Social Security account you will select Yes and then click the Next button. You will now be directed to the sign in page. Once signed in, simply enter the required information.

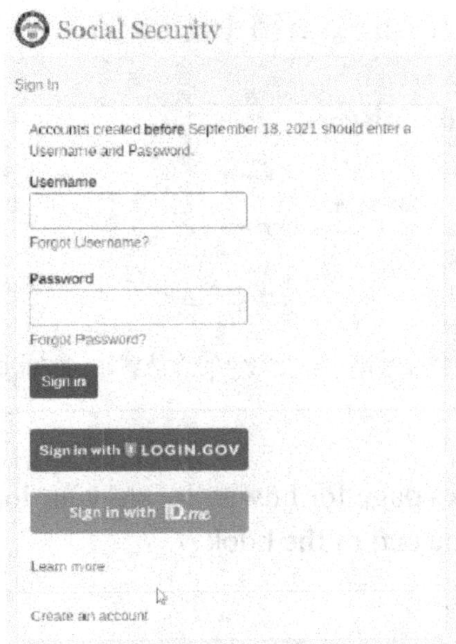

FEELING A BIT OVERWHELMED?

No worries! You can simply make an appointment at your local Social Security office. Keep in mind that some local offices with a large senior population can be booked out 2-3 months, so it is important to act sooner than later. It is advisable to use the IEP calculator to see when your optimal enrollment dates are and then try scheduling an appointment during that time period.

The 3 enrollment periods

1. When you're turning 65

This is the "Initial Enrollment Period," and there are no penalties if you sign up during this time.

Enter your birth date to see when you can first enroll:

Select month ∨	Select day ∨	Select year ∨

www.ssa.gov/medicare/plan/when-to-sign-up

View our **Resources** page for how to locate your local Social Security office at the end of the book.

CHAPTER 8:
When to Enroll in Medicare

WHEN TO ENROLL IN MEDICARE

For most folks the best time to enroll in Medicare is during your Initial Enrollment Period (IEP) which is a 7-month period made up of the following:

- 3 months prior to your birthday month when turning 65
- Your birthday month when turning 65
- 3 months after your birthday month of when you turned 65

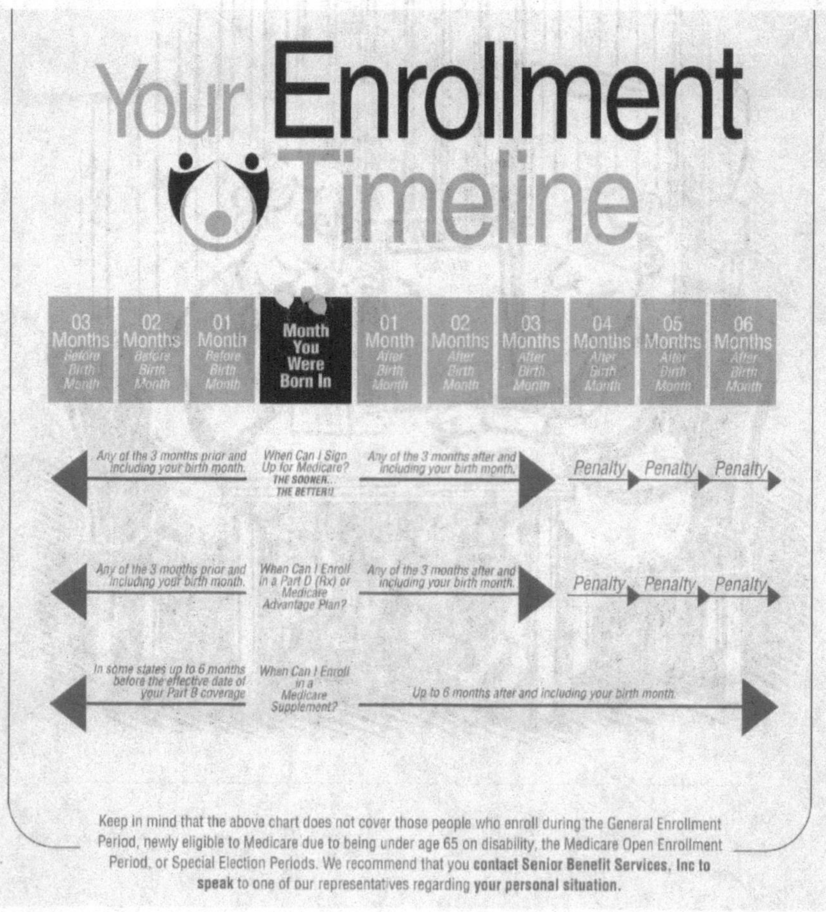

While this might be the best time for most folks, there are instances when this might not be best for you. Let's look at some of these particular situations.

- You work for a large employer (has 20 or more employees) and want to continue working past age 65. You can go ahead and sign up for Part A in this situation and delay Medicare Parts B and D. The large employer group health plan would be primary (pays first), and your Medicare Part A would be secondary (pays second). Important: If you have an HSA plan that you are contributing to and want to continue contributing to, you should delay Medicare Part A as well. You should also be aware that when you eventually enroll in Part A of Medicare, Social Security will make your effective date retroactive by six months prior to the application date. Because of this, it is best to stop making contributions to your health savings account at least 6 months prior to making your application for Medicare. To review other specific employer situations, the Centers for Medicare and Medicaid Studies (CMS) have published a guide. Simply go to www.medicare.gov & search for Publication 11546 Coordination of Benefits. Download & view as PDF. Request hard copy from CMS.

It is very important that if you choose to delay Medicare Part D that your employer group health plan meets the definition of having credible prescription drug coverage. You should first ask your HR department if the current plan meets the guidelines. If it does not, then you will want to enroll in a Medicare Part D prescription drug plan so that you are not dealing with a lifetime penalty down the road.

Important: Each year you should receive from your HR Department or insurance company a letter stating the group prescription drug benefit is considered 'credible coverage'. It is highly advised that you save these notices.

Discount prescription plans are not recognized by Medicare as being credible coverage. While they can be beneficial, they are not actual insurance.

- You work for a small employer (has less than 20 employees) and want to continue working past age 65. In this situation you will want to sign up for both Medicare Parts A and B when turning 65. Medicare will be your primary coverage, and your small group plan will act as your supplement and pay secondary. It is important for you to review the costs of your small group health plan to see if you should stick with it or obtain new health insurance coverage (a Medicare Supplement or Medicare Advantage plan with integrated prescription drug coverage) and a Part D prescription drug plan if choosing to enroll in a Medicare Supplement. The reality is that in many situations the cost to remain on a small employer group health plan can be far more expensive than other alternatives.
- You receive health insurance coverage in retirement as part of your benefits package. While fewer and fewer companies are providing this, if you are one of the lucky ones, then you will still need to enroll into Medicare Parts A and B.
- You have federal coverage such as TRICARE for Life (TFL) or Federal Employee Health Benefits (FEHB).

If you have one of these plans you usually do not need to purchase any additional supplemental coverage.

1. TRICARE - this is the health program for retired military personnel. Medicare will be primary (so you will still need to sign up for Parts A and B) and the TRICARE plan will act as your supplemental coverage. In other words, TRICARE will mimic the benefits of a Medicare Supplement plan.

2. FEHB - the simple thing for you to know is that you do not need to purchase a Medicare Supplement or Medicare Advantage plan. If you have FEHB and want to understand more about how it coordinates with Medicare, you should visit the Office of Personnel Management's website at www.opm.gov at the top of the page in the search box, simply type in coordination of Medicare benefits then press enter on your keyboard and this will bring up the publication titled "Coordination of Medicare and FEHB Benefits".

I would be remiss in not at least mentioning Continuation of Health Coverage (COBRA)

While this might be the best time for most folks, there are instances when this might not be best for you. Let's look at some of these particular situations.

COBRA requires that large employer groups provide their employees the possibility of extending their health coverage in situations where the employee would otherwise lose coverage under the plan. This is available to employees who have lost or will be losing their employment-based insurance due to certain qualifying events such as reduction in work hours, termination of employment, and divorce or legal separation. It is also available in cases of death of the employee, when coverage for dependent children would otherwise end due to their age or other circumstances. COBRA provides employees with a temporary extension of health insurance coverage at group rates, allowing them to maintain their existing plan and avoid having to purchase an individual policy on the market. This can be a valuable safety net for employees who may need to bridge the gap between jobs, or who are unable to find an individual policy that meets their needs.

However, COBRA is not a long-term solution, and coverage typically ends after 18 months. In addition, COBRA is not recognized as credible coverage by Medicare.

Important: If you become eligible for Medicare while covered under COBRA, you must still elect to enroll in Medicare, or you will face a penalty later.

CHAPTER 9:
Avoiding the Medicare Part D Penalty

AVOIDING THE MEDICARE PART D PENALTY

One of the top questions our company gets each year from those aging into Medicare is "Do I really need to buy a Part D prescription drug plan to go along with my Medicare Supplement?" The answer is YES! You may be saying to yourself, "well if I am not taking any medications why should I spend the money?" The answer to this is very simple, if you do not enroll in a Part D plan when you first become eligible you will incur a lifetime penalty that is 1% for each month you delay from the time you were first eligible. Also, you cannot simply enroll later at any time that you want. You must wait until the Annual Enrollment Period (AEP) which runs from October 15th –December 7th each year. While you can enroll during this period, the prescription drug coverage will still not go into effect until January 1st of the next year.

Example: Jane is turning 65 and enrolls in Medicare Parts A and B. She then purchases a Medicare Supplement Plan G to make sure she is well protected. Jane is contemplating on whether or not to enroll in a Part D plan since she does not take any prescriptions. After a period of time dwelling on this, Jane decides not to enroll in a Part D plan. Over the years Jane starts to see her blood pressure going a little bit higher each year. Finally, after 4 years since she went on Medicare, her doctor puts her on a blood pressure medication. While the medication is not very expensive, Jane begins to worry she might end up on more prescriptions as she continues to age. Jane decides it's time to get a Part D prescription drug plan. Since she has gone 4 years without one since first eligible, she will encounter a 1% simple penalty for each month. This means that Jane will now pay a 48% penalty each month. The penalty amount is also not based on the lowest priced Part D plan available in Jane's zip code but based off the national base premium. In 2026 the national base premium is $38.99 per month. To compute Jane's penalty, it would look something like this:

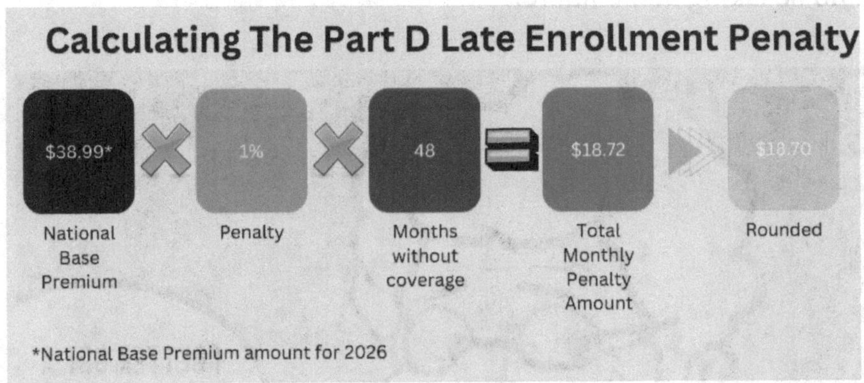

Now let's assume that the plan that works best for Jane is priced at $22.00 per month.

$22.00 + $18.70 (rounded to nearest $0.10) = $40.70 is what Jane will pay for that plan due to the penalty.

It is important to note that the penalty will follow Jane for the rest of her life and will recalculate each year based on what the national base premium is.

So, what should Jane have done differently. When she first became eligible to enroll in a Medicare Part D plan, she could have simply enrolled in the lowest priced plan. Many times, these plans are around $7.00 - $10.00 per month which is cheaper than the penalty she will now be paying. Besides avoiding the penalty, Jane would have had coverage in place just in case she was put onto a prescription mid-year.

Think of it this way, you are purchasing a prescription drug plan to not only cover what you are currently taking but more so for what you could be taking in the future.

CHAPTER 10:
Understanding the Phases of a Prescription Plan

UNDERSTANDING THE PHASES OF A PRESCRIPTION PLAN

When you first start looking at Part D prescription plans and how they work, it is quite intimidating. In fact most folks think that when they are going onto Medicare and sign up for a Part D plan that it works just like their prescription plan did with their group insurance. Sorry to say...that is not the case. Before we get into the phases of a Part D prescription drug plan, it is important to know a couple of basic things:

1. You can only have one Part D prescription drug plan.
2. If you enroll in a Medicare Advantage Plan that has an integrated drug plan, then you cannot also enroll in a separate Part D plan.

UNDERSTANDING THE PHASES OF PART D

Each time you reach a spending threshold you will enter a new phase of your plan. These phases include:

- The Deductible
- The Initial Coverage Phase
- The Catastrophic Coverage Phase

To make this a bit easier to understand, please see the chart below.

<u>Medicare Part D Prescription Drug Plan</u>

*Breaking Down The Costs
For Year*

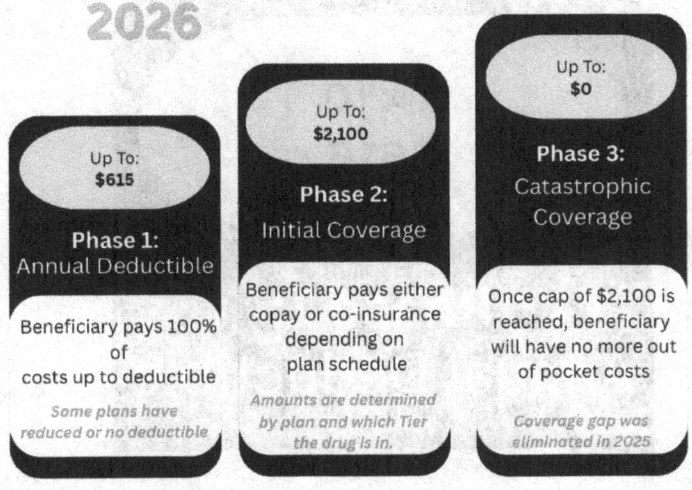

When you first start looking at Part D prescription plans and how they work, it is quite intimidating. In fact most folks think that when they are going onto Medicare and sign up for a Part D plan that it works just like their prescription plan did with their group insurance. Sorry to say...that is not the case.

The first thing to understand is that each year Medicare will establish the maximum drug deductible that a Part D plan can have. An insurance company cannot decide to make their deductible higher than the maximum set by Medicare for that year. While they cannot make their deductible higher, some plans choose to set a lower deductible or even no deductible at all. Many times this will be reflected in them charging a higher monthly premium than other Part D carriers.

For 2026 the annual deductible for Phase 1 has been set at $615

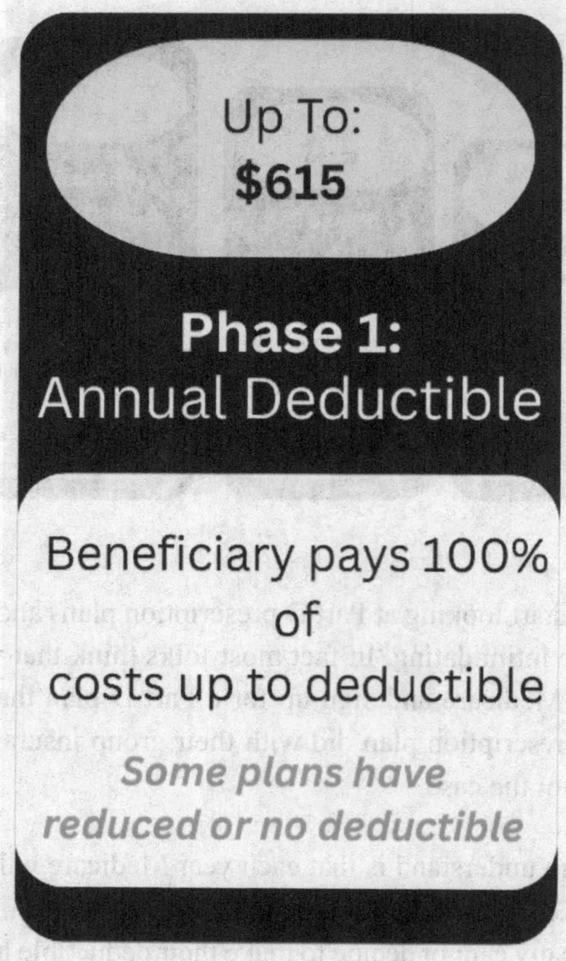

During Phase 1 you are simply paying the full price of the prescription and that amount is being applied towards your annual deductible. So exactly how does this work? Using the example below we will move thru Phase 1.

Example: Jane has just enrolled in her Medicare Part D prescription drug plan, and it has the full maximum deductible of $615. The first prescription that Jane needs to have filled is her hypertension medication. The retail price for this prescription is $98. Jane will be responsible for paying the full $98 at the pharmacy and this amount will be applied to her deductible.

$615 (annual deductible) - $98 (Rx retail cost) = $517

The following month Jane's thyroid medication is due to be refilled, and the retail cost of that drug is $175. Jane will once again be responsible for paying the full $175 at the pharmacy and this amount will also be applied towards her deductible.

$517 (remaining annual deductible) - $175 (Rx retail cost) = $342

The very next week Jane has to also get her cholesterol medication refilled. The retail price for this prescription is $85. Jane will be responsible for paying the full $85 at the pharmacy once again and this amount will be applied to her deductible.

$342 (remaining annual deductible) - $85 (Rx retail cost) = $257

Since Jane is now in her second month, she needs to get her hypertension medication refilled. Since she has not met the annual deductible yet for the year, the full amount of $98 will once again be paid at the pharmacy and applied to her remaining deductible amount.

$257 (remaining annual deductible) - $98 (Rx retail cost) = $159

The following month Jane's thyroid medication needs to be refilled. Instead of the full retail pricing being paid at the pharmacy she will only pay the remaining part of her annual deductible and whatever the co-pay amount is for that drug since she will be entering Phase 2.

After Jane refills her Thyroid medication the deductible will have been met.

Jane's deductible has now been met for the year, and she will now move into Phase 2 when she refills her next prescription.

IMPORTANT: If Jane were enrolled in a prescription plan that did not have a deductible, then she would simply start in Phase 2 making co-payments.

It is also important to keep in mind that many plans now offer preferred pricing on certain medications during the deductible phase. This means your costs may be lower. To gain further knowledge on which plan would be suitable for your personal needs, it is advisable to speak to one of our advisors.

The Initial Coverage Phase – Phase 2

During the initial coverage phase your costs will fall into one of two categories. The first category is a co-payment which is a flat dollar amount. The second category is co-insurance which is a percentage of the prescription price. Once again Medicare establishes the limit for the initial coverage phase.

So how is this phase calculated? Unlike Phase 1 where you were responsible for the full amount of the prescription costs to reach the deductible, in Phase 2 the amount you pay in either co-pays or co-insurance, along with amounts covered by the manufacturer and the plan are all added together to count towards your Phase 2 limit.

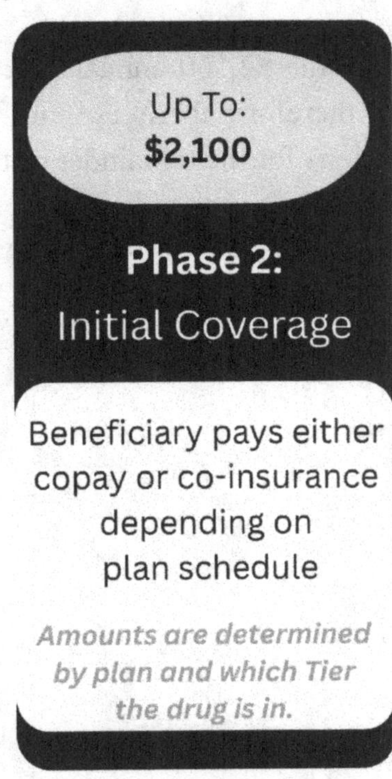

Many seniors never exit out of Phase 2 since quite a number of medications that are prescribed today are generics which have a lower cost to them. So for 2026 the Initial Coverage Phase is the amount between $615-$2,100.

If you are taking a generic that has a $10 co-pay, but the overall cost of the drug is $90, that full amount is applied towards your initial coverage limit. Keep in mind that you will only pay the $10 co-payment out of pocket.

The Catastrophic Phase – Phase 3

Once you reach Phase 3 the $2,100 annual maximum out of pocket has been reached so therefore there are no more out-of-pocket costs for your prescriptions for the remainder of the calendar year.

You will begin the same process over beginning January 1st of each year.

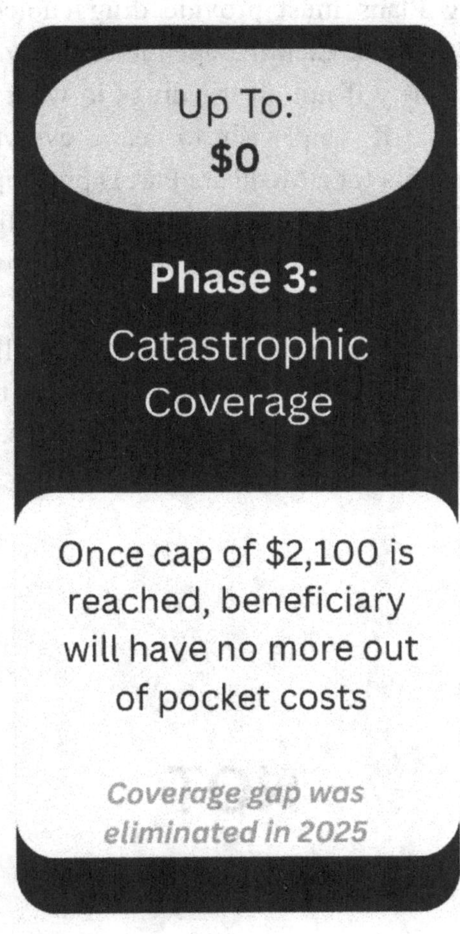

IMPORTANT: The following do NOT count towards your TrOOP:4

- Your monthly premiums paid to the insurance company for your prescription plan coverage.
- Any prescriptions you choose to get that are not covered by the plan's formulary.

Prescription Drug Plans must provide drug choices of at least 2 different prescriptions for each therapeutic category. The plans must also cover the majority if not all the drugs in what is referred to as 'critical categories'. If you wish to learn everything about the minimum requirements for a Medicare Part D prescription drug plan's formulary, you can go to www.cms.gov and then click on Medicare, scroll down until you see the heading Prescription Drug Coverage and then click on the hyperlink for Prescription Drug Coverage Contracting. On the left side of your screen you will see a hyperlink titled Prescription Drug Benefit Manual. Click on that hyperlink to bring you to the downloads section where you can select Chapter 6 – Part D Drugs and Formulary Requirements.

Now that we have covered what the Part D plans must cover, let's look at things that the plans typically will not. These are not in any particular order:

- Drugs designed to help with weight issues.
- Drugs to treat cosmetic issues.
- Drugs that fall into the sedatives category
- Prescribed Vitamins
- Over The Counter Medications

CHAPTER 11:
Choosing the Right
Part D Plan

Choosing the Right Part D Plan

There is more to choosing a Medicare Part D prescription drug plan than just simply going with the lowest monthly premium. Let's look at some of the key areas that you need to understand.

Formulary – A drug formulary is a list of medications that are approved for use by an individual health plan or organization. It helps to ensure that patients receive the best possible care while also controlling costs. A formulary typically includes name brand and generic drugs, along with preferred drugs and those in different dosage forms so that prescribers have cost-effective options available when prescribing medications.

When reviewing a plan's formulary, it is also vital to review if there are any limitations on your current prescriptions. We classify plan limitations to include such things as:

- **Prior Authorization** – This requirement means that before the pharmacy can fill this prescription, you will need your doctor to obtain approval from the drug plan. Just because the insurance coverage that you are moving from may already approve this prescription, it will have no bearing on whether or not the new plan will. The burden will fall on your doctor to show why this particular medication must be used by you compared to a lower costing alternative.

- **Step Therapy** – When a plan requires step therapy, they are requiring you to try out lower costing alternative prescriptions first rather than simply approving you to fill the higher costing one. If your doctor can show thru previous documentation that you have already tried these cheaper alternatives and they did not work, then you can file for a drug exception request to bypass step therapy. Once again, this is not guaranteed but is definitely worth the try.

Important Tip: First always look for a drug plan that covers all your prescription drugs within its formulary, otherwise you will be paying 100% of the costs for those drugs not on it.

- **Quantity Limits** – This is when the drug plan limits the amount of the medication that it will cover for each refill. These prescriptions are usually either extremely expensive or fall into a category that could make them unsafe (i.e., easily addictive). You will almost always see this limitation when it comes to addictive pain medications such as Oxycodone.

R

Name: _______________________
DOB: _______________________
Phone: _______________________
Address: _______________________

PRESCRIPTION:

90 day supply

Do not refill ☐
Refill ___ times

_______________   _______________
Date   Signature

Overall Costs – This is why you do not simply look for the cheapest plan available in your area (unless you are currently on no prescriptions). Your overall costs include such things as:

- Your total monthly premiums for the year.
- Your annual deductible.
- Your co-pays and co-insurance that you pay at the pharmacy or thru mail order when refilling your prescriptions.

- Your costs while moving through Phases 2-3
- Any additional costs for a particular prescription not covered by any plan.
- Last but not least, the plan's ratings.

CHAPTER 12:
Choices...Choices and More CHOICES

Choices…. Choices and More CHOICES

Let's start with one of the first choices you have to make with Medicare. Do you have to pay for Part B, or can you simply save the money each month? This is a loaded question!

Since Part B of Medicare is typically deducted right out of your social security check each month, the federal government cannot require you to pay it. Part B of Medicare is not FREE. Now, before you go and start thinking of how much extra money you will have each month it is important to understand that if you opt to go without Part B of Medicare you will face the following issues:

- Have absolutely no coverage for doctors, surgeons, outpatient surgery centers or other outpatient services. This is a very dangerous gamble and one we would never recommend a retiree to even consider.
- You cannot enroll in a Medicare Supplement plan.
- You cannot enroll in a Medicare Advantage plan.

Now you see why this is a loaded question. While the government cannot require you to have Part B and pay for it, you will end up leaving yourself financially exposed to a point that you could become financially devasted by a severe medical condition. So having and paying for Part B really is not an option for retirees.

The next choice that you will face is deciding whether or not you want to remain in traditional Medicare (Parts A & B) or enroll in Part C (Medicare Advantage). One of the most common misconceptions about Part C of Medicare is that you wouldn't have to continue to pay for Part B if you were to enroll in a Medicare Advantage plan. This is not the case. **You must still pay your monthly Part B premiums even if you decide to enroll in a Medicare Advantage plan!**

If you choose to remain in original Medicare, you will want to then choose a Medicare Supplement plan to cover the deductibles and co-insurance amounts not covered by Medicare Parts A & B. In addition, you will need to choose a stand-alone Medicare Part D prescription drug plan (PDP).

For those who choose to enroll in a Medicare Advantage plan, you will definitely want to make sure it is one that has an integrated drug benefit built into the plan unless you have credible prescription drug coverage benefits somewhere else. A Medicare Advantage plan with built in prescription benefits is known as an MAPD. Many retirees who have access to Veteran's benefits will get their prescriptions filled at the local VA Hospital. If you have access to that benefit, then you can enroll in a Medicare Advantage plan without prescriptions benefits which is known simply as a MA plan.5 See Diagram on next page.

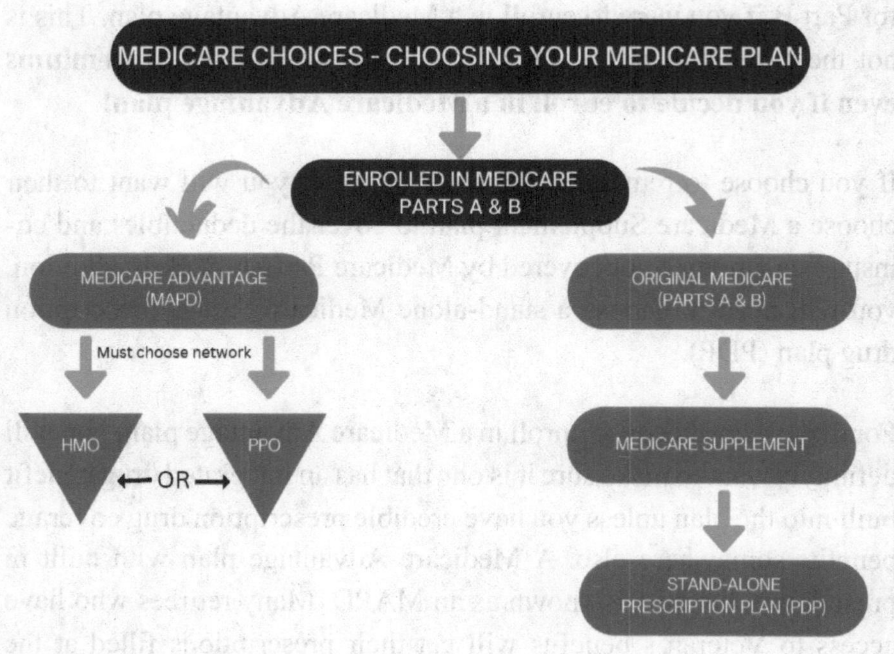

MEDICARE CHOICES - CHOOSING YOUR MEDICARE PLAN
ENROLLED IN MEDICARE
PARTS A & B
MEDICARE ADVANTAGE
(MAPD)
ORIGINAL MEDICARE
(PARTS A & B)
Must choose network
MEDICARE SUPPLEMENT
HMO
PPO
← OR →
STAND-ALONE
PRESCRIPTION PLAN (PDP)

CHAPTER 13:
What You Need to Know When Choosing Original Medicare

What You Need to Know When Choosing Original Medicare

When you really look at the benefits you receive thru original Medicare, they are quite generous. With original Medicare you simply need to see a provider who accepts Medicare (which is the majority). There are no networks to worry about, no referrals required, and prior authorization is not required for the vast majority of services. In other words, traditional Medicare offers great flexibility.

Keep in mind that traditional Medicare does not cover everything and that you will be responsible for such things as certain deductibles, co-payments and co-insurance under each part. See figure 5 for current costs.

Figure 5

Your Medicare Costs 2026

Part A Deductible and Coinsurance
You Pay:
$1736 deductible for each benefit period
Days 1-60:
$0 coinsurance for each benefit period
Days 61-90:
$434 coinsurance per day of each benefit period
Days 91 and beyond:
$868 coinsurance per each "lifetime reserve day" (up to a maximum of 60 days). Once lifetime reserve days used: ALL COSTS

Skilled Nursing
First 20 days covered 100% by Medicare
You pay **$217 per day for days 21-100**

Part B Deductible and Coinsurance
$283 for the year **PLUS 20%** of the Medicare approved amount

Part B Excess Charges
Medicare pays $0
You pay **100%**

The remaining exposure can be covered partially or almost in its entirety thru a Medicare Supplement plan or sometimes referred to as a Medigap plan.

Important Tip: It is easy to become confused with all the letters that we are using. As you can see from the chart above, there are Medicare Supplement plans which use the same letters as what we see under Medicare itself. The easiest way to avoid the confusion is to remember that the term PARTS always will be used with Medicare and the term PLANS will always be used with Medicare Supplements.

While there is a total of 12 standardized plans, most new to Medicare beneficiaries choose either a Plan N or Plan G for their Medicare Supplement plan. Since January 1, 2020, those new to Medicare can no longer purchase a Plan C or Plan F.

In addition to choosing a Medicare Supplement plan you will need to decide on a Medicare Part D (PDP) prescription drug plan. Choosing a stand-alone Part D plan will allow you to enroll in a plan that will provide you with the most coverage with the lowest annual out-of-pocket costs.

While making these key decisions when opting to stay in original Medicare, you will have given yourself the most flexible coverage, but not necessarily the cheapest.

CHAPTER 14:
What You Need to Know When Choosing Medicare Advantage

What You Need to Know When Choosing Medicare Advantage

Many retirees are drawn to Medicare Advantage plans due to their low monthly premiums. The easiest way to explain why these plans cost far less than a Medicare Supplement plan is to understand that you are sharing the medical costs each time with the insurance company. Medicare Advantage plans are what we refer to as "Pay As You Play or Pay As You Go" plans. In addition to sharing costs thru co-payments and co-insurance, you will need to navigate through other cost saving features that the plan could use.

Networks – as we discussed before Medicare Advantage plans typically will use either a Preferred Provider Organization network (PPO) or a Health Maintenance Organization network (HMO) to reduce costs to the insurance company. So how do these networks differ?

- **HMO** – this is the most restrictive type of network. For you to have benefits paid, you must use a provider that participates with this particular network. If the provider does not participate and you choose to be seen by them anyway, you will be responsible for 100% of the costs.
- **PPO** – this type of network is a bit less restrictive in the fact that it allows you to see a provider not in the network. It is important to understand that seeing providers within the network will lower your out-of-pocket costs such as having a lower co-pay. Seeing a provider outside of the network will have not only larger co-pays but will typically result in additional out-of-pocket costs since they will be

paid less by the plan. Additionally, most PPO plans have separate deductibles and maximum out-of-pocket costs for in-network and out-of-network expenses.

Maximum Out of Pocket (MOOP) – this is the maximum amount of expenses that you would pay for out of your own pocket in a calendar year. Most plans have an in-network MOOP of around $7,500 while the out-of-network MOOP is around $10,000 for the calendar year.

Important Tip: It is important to remember that any expenses counted towards the MOOP for in-network expenses do not get applied to the out-of-network MOOP (and vice versa). In addition, your prescription expenses under the integrated drug coverage portion of the plan does NOT count towards the MOOP.

Referrals – many Medicare Advantage plans will first require you to choose a primary care physician (PCP) who will oversee aspects of your care. This means that unlike being in traditional Medicare you will need to get a referral from your PCP to see a specialist. For many tests you would need to obtain prior authorization.6

Important Tip: You can always view what your plan requirements and out-of-pocket costs are prior to enrolling. This information is provided in the Summary of Benefits that is required to be provided to you by law.

Integrated Drug Coverage – unlike a stand-alone Part D plan where you can look for one that covers all your prescriptions in their formulary, a Medicare Advantage plan has its own dedicated formulary. This means that if the plan doesn't cover your prescription, then you will be responsible to pay for that out of your own pocket each month. While some folks will enroll in the plan anyway and then file an exception with the plan asking them to cover the prescription, there is no guarantee that the plan will approve the exception. If the prescription is not that expensive and the plan will not cover it, then you might simply choose to pay for that medication out of pocket while still enrolling into the plan. We typically advise our clients to enroll in a plan that covers all their prescriptions to reduce their overall MOOP for the calendar year.

Unless you have been living under a rock for the last 10 years, you have seen at least one Medicare Advantage commercial on television. While most of these have been seen as misleading, they do typically tout having what are known as "Extra Benefits". Some of these extra benefits can include:

- Routine Dental
- Routine Vision
- Routine Hearing
- Gym memberships

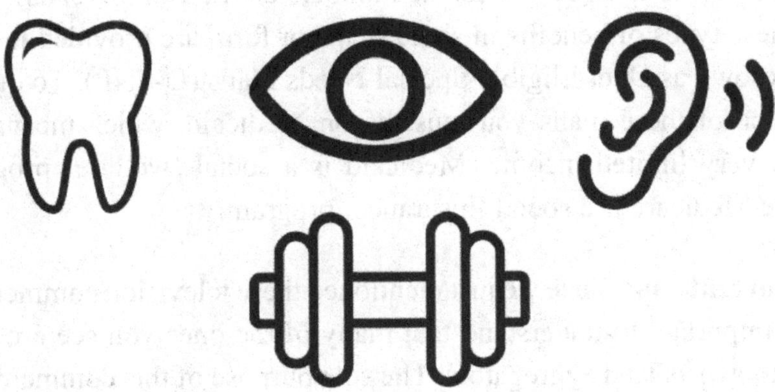

While these extra benefits sound great on paper, they typically come with network restrictions and/or limited value. An example of this would be dental benefits. Most retirees already have a favorite dentist, but to access this extra dental benefit, that dentist usually must be part of the plan's network. So, if your favorite dentist is not part of the network, you will need to pick a new dentist out of the plan's network listing. Additionally, this benefit may have a maximum annual value that is not really worth all the hassle of giving up your current dentist.

What about the additional benefits that say will pay me up to $3,400 per year and give me a bunch of additional free items. Sorry to say that very few folks actually qualify for these benefits (but they sure do entice people to call those phone numbers on the commercials). Most of these types of benefits in some shape or form are provided in what are known as Duel Eligible Special Needs Plans (D-SNP). To qualify for one of these plans you must be on Medicaid, which means you have very limited income. Medicaid is a social 'welfare' program, while Medicare is a social 'insurance' program.

Important Tip: Since we just mentioned these television commercials it is important to understand that many of the ones you see are what are known as lead aggregators. The sole purpose of this commercial is to get you to call in and then you are transferred to either a call center or some random agent that has paid for 'this lead'. The lead aggregator makes their money from the call center/agent buying the lead, so therefore the call center/agent is concerned with making their money back as quickly as possible. They are focused on trying to enroll you into a Medicare Advantage plan to make a commission. You are not going to get an agent that will take the time to explain all your Medicare options and help you determine if a Medicare Advantage plan or Medicare Supplement plan makes more sense for your personal situation. In fact, their goal is to enroll you as quickly as possible so they can take another call and hopefully make another sale.

Additional Key Points

- As we discussed earlier, you must be enrolled first in Medicare Parts A & B to qualify to enroll in a Medicare Advantage plan.
- Must continue to pay your monthly Medicare Part B premium.
- You can only enroll in a Medicare Advantage plan if it is available in the zip code where you permanently reside. This means that if a plan is available in the county next to the one you live in, but not in your county itself, you cannot enroll in the plan. Easiest way to understand this is that if it is not showing in your zip code, then you cannot enroll in it.
- A Medicare Advantage plan is not guaranteed renewable like a Medicare Supplement plan. This means that an insurance company can choose at the end of the year not to offer a plan or particular plan in your county. If this occurs, Medicare will provide what is called a Special Enrollment

Period (SEP) to choose another plan or return to original Medicare. If a Medicare Supplement insurance company chooses to no longer sell new plans in a state, the company must still service and pay claims for those policyholders. Their coverage is guaranteed renewable for as long as they pay their premiums on time.

- No matter what you are told, a physician is not required to join a plan's network. If a physician is part of the network, they can choose to leave the network mid-year if they choose. If your doctor leaves the plan network, this does not give you an opportunity to leave the plan as well. If you have been in a Medicare Advantage plan already for a calendar year, then you will have to remain in the plan until the end of the current contract year.

- You do have a trial right when you first join a Medicare Advantage plan. This means that when you first become eligible for Medicare (let's assume age 65) and you join a Medicare Advantage plan right out of the gate, you will have up to a 12-month period to change your mind. If you exercise this trial right, then you can move back to original Medicare, enroll in a Part D prescription drug plan, and even apply for a Medicare Supplement plan with no underwriting.7

CHAPTER 15:
What You Need to Know When Choosing Medicare Supplement

What You Need to Know When Choosing Medicare Supplement

Since 1992 Medicare Supplement plans have been standardized. This means that if you compare the plan benefits of a Plan G with one carrier, to another carrier, they must be the same. This means that you are now comparing the following areas:

- Monthly premium Carrier ratings
- Carrier rate increase history
- Rating methodology (attained age, issue age, community rated)

What caused plans to become standardized? Prior to 1992, plans typically only needed to have what were referred to as core or basic benefits. Everything else that you would want could be purchased as a rider. The problem with this is that many times retirees thought that they had certain benefits, when in fact their plan did not have that rider selected. Sorry to say that there were also a number of insurance agents 'bad apples' that used this confusion to get a person to purchase a plan from them. They would tell the consumer that the price of their plan was not only lower than their competition but also covered those additional benefits when they did not. The standardization helped to eliminate a number of these folks which we were very happy to see leave our industry.

Important Tip: If you live in Wisconsin, Minnesota, or Massachusetts you will not have standardized plans. You will have base plans that you can add riders to that will resemble many of the standardized plans.

Over the years we have seen new plans developed and outdated plans replaced.

The chart below shows all current standardized plans.

MEDIGAP PLANS 2026

BENEFITS FOR EACH PLAN	A	B	D	G*	K	L	M	N		C	F*
Medicare Part A coinsurance and hospital costs (up to an additional 365 days after Medicare benefits are used)	100%	100%	100%	100%	100%	100%	100%	100%		100%	100%
Medicare Part B coinsurance or copayment	100%	100%	100%	100%	50%	75%	100%	100%***		100%	100%
Part A hospice care coinsurance or copayment	100%	100%	100%	100%	50%	75%	100%	100%		100%	100%
Skilled nursing facility care coinsurance		100%	100%	100%	50%	75%	100%	100%		100%	100%
Part A deductible		100%	100%	100%	50%	75%	50%	100%		100%	100%
Part B deductible										100%	100%
Part B excess charges				100%							100%
Foreign travel emergency (up to plan limits)			80%	80%			80%	80%		80%	80%
Out-of-Pocket Limit in 2026**					$8,000	$4,000					

Medigap Plans Available Before 2020 ONLY

How do I compare Medigap plans? The chart above shows basic information about the different benefits that Medicare Supplement Insurance (Medigap) plans cover for 2026. If a percentage appears, the Medigap plan covers that percentage of the benefit, and you're responsible for the rest. Out-of-pocket costs (like deductibles) might change for 2027.

* Plans F and G also offer a high-deductible plan in some states. With this option, you must pay for Medicare-covered costs (coinsurance, copayments, and deductibles) up to the deductible amount of $2,950 in 2026 before your policy pays anything. (You can't buy Plans C and F if you were newly eligible for Medicare on or after January 1, 2020. See the previous page for more information.)

** For Plans K and L, after you meet your out-of-pocket yearly limit and your yearly Part B deductible ($283 in 2026), the Medigap plan pays 100% of covered services for the rest of the calendar year.

*** Plan N pays 100% of the Part B coinsurance. You must pay a copayment of up to $20 for some office visits and up to a $50 copayment for emergency room visits that don't result in an inpatient admission.

With this many plans available, it is no wonder that many folks are overwhelmed with just choosing a Medicare Supplement plan. Prior to January 1, 2020, the most popular plan was a Plan F. Since anyone who is new to Medicare after this date cannot purchase a Plan F, the Plan G became the obvious replacement.

As you can see below, the only difference between the 2 plans is that the Plan G does not cover the annual Part B deductible which is $283 for 2026.

Which is the Best Plan: F vs G

MEDIGAP PLANS BENEFITS	F	G
Medicare Part A Coinsurance and Hospital Costs (up to an additional 365 days after Medicare benefits are used)	✓	✓
Medicare Part B Coinsurance or Copayment	✓	✓
Blood (first 3 pints)	✓	✓
Medicare Part A Hospice Care Coinsurance or Copayment	✓	✓
Skilled Nursing Facility Care Coinsurance	✓	✓
Medicare Part A Deductible	✓	✓
Medicare Part B Deductible	✓	✗
Medicare Part B Excess Charges	✓	✓
Foreign Travel Emergency (up to plan limit)	✓	✓

Plan G

Is Plan G the cheapest Medicare Supplement plan available? Absolutely not. In fact, it is usually one of the higher priced plans. The reason for this is that it leaves little out of pocket costs to the policyholder.

Let's take a real-world example and see why this is the case with the example on the next page:

Joan decides on enrolling into a Medicare Supplement Plan G. On January 1st she goes to see her family doctor. Joan happens to suffer from one of leading illnesses in the United States…diabetes. While Joan has been diligent at keeping her Type II diabetes under control (with the help of diet, exercise, and one oral medication, she still needs to have blood work and lab tests completed. The good news is that after Joan covers her first $283 in Part B expenses, Medicare is going to cover 80% of the approved charges and her Plan G will cover the rest. For the remaining part of the year, Joan no longer has any additional expenses coming out of her pocket since she has met her Part B annual deductible of $283 for 2026. Under Part A her plan covers not only her hospital deductible but all the daily co-pays she would need to cover if she had an extended stay in the hospital.

In addition to all these benefits, Joan also receives coverage for foreign travel emergency benefits outside the United States with her Plan G. An additional benefit built into the Plan G is coverage for excess charges. While most providers accept Medicare assignment there are a few who choose to balance bill their patients by an additional 15% above what Medicare approves. If Joan were to see one of these providers (including surgeons those additional charges would be covered at 100% with her Plan G.

Even though Medicare Supplement plans typically cost more than Medicare Advantage plans, why do folks still choose them? The answer really is quite simple….NO FINANCIAL SURPRISES!

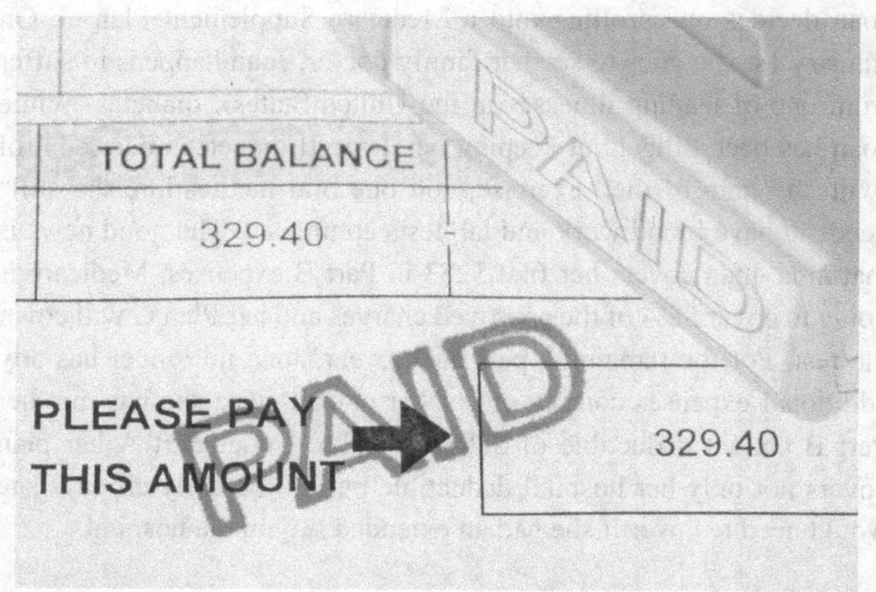

Let's say that Joan's Plan G costs $120 per month (rates vary). If we take her Part B annual deductible for 2026 (which is $283) and divide that up over a 12-month period, Joan knows that her health insurance cost is $143.58 per month (monthly premium+ Part B deductible) even if she ends up seeing a bunch of doctors or has hospital stays for multiple days or multiple times within the same year. This allows Joan to easily budget her monthly expenses.

Important Tip: Since Medicare Advantage plans are 'pay as you go', the insured really does not have a monthly fixed cost. One month it could just be the low monthly premium being paid out, and the next month could be a $300 per day daily hospital co-pay for 4 days ($1,200 out-of-pocket).

Is there a solid Medicare Supplement plan available that is not as expensive as the Plan G? Yes! Many folks who still want to have the flexibility that traditional Medicare and a Medicare Supplement afford them, find that a Plan N works really well for them.

Plan N

The Plan N typically does cost less per month than a Plan G in most states. There are some key points when it comes to benefits that make the Plan N what we call a 'hybrid' type of plan due to having some co-pays. To see a side-by-side comparison of benefits between the Plan N and Plan G see the chart below.

Benefits	Plan G	Plan N
Basic benefits under Part A including daily coinsurance for days 60-150. Up to an additional 365 days after day 150.	✓	✓
Part A Deductible	✓	✓
Skilled Nursing Facility Daily Coinsurance	✓	✓
Part A Hospice Care	✓	✓
Blood (Pints 1-3)	✓	✓
Medicare Part B Coinsurance	✓	✓ *
Medicare Part B Deductible	✗	✗
Foreign Travel (Emergency Benefits)	✓	✓
Medicare Part B Excess Charges	✓	✗

As you can see from the benefit comparison you will still need to cover the annual Part B deductible first. After the deductible has been met, Medicare will once again typically cover 80% of the approved amounts, but you will have co-pays of up to $20 for certain types of doctor visits and up to a $50 co-pay for emergency room visits. The other benefit difference between Plan N and Plan G is that while Plan G covers excess charges, the Plan N does not. Since the majority of providers accept what Medicare approves, excess charges very rarely come into play.

Important Tip: One way to easily avoid excess charges is to simply ask the provider if they accept Medicare Assignment (which means they don't charge excess charges/balance bill).

CHAPTER 16:
Medicare Supplement Enrollment Periods

Medicare Supplement Enrollment Periods

Open Enrollment (OEP)

This is commonly a one-time enrollment period, so it is important not to miss it! I cannot stress enough that this is a very important period, and you do not receive this each year. Many folks confuse this with the Medicare enrollment period that runs from October 15th – December 7th which allows you to make changes to a Medicare Advantage plan or Part D prescription drug plan.

When you enroll in Medicare Part B you will have a one-time enrollment period where you can enroll in a Medicare Supplement with absolutely NO UNDERWRITING. This is very important since many folks going onto Medicare have pre-existing health conditions, and some can be really serious. This Open Enrollment Period is 6 months long that starts when you first enroll in Part B of Medicare.

Missing The Medicare Supplement Open Enrollment Period

If you were to somehow miss this enrollment period, you would now need to answer the medical/health questions on the application. You would not get the coverage automatically but rather you would have to medically qualify. This would be the same situation if years down the road you decided to switch insurance companies for your Medicare Supplement. Once again you would have to medically qualify for them to issue you a plan.

Important Tip: You can actually start shopping for your Medicare Supplement plan prior to your Part B effective date. In many states you can actually enroll in a Medicare Supplement plan (to be effective the same day as your Part B) up to six months prior. Some folks do this to go ahead and get everything out of the way, while most typically do the enrollment 3-4 months prior to their Part B effective date.

I would be remiss if I did not at least address why I stated that the Medicare Supplement Open Enrollment Period is 'commonly a one-time' occurrence. There is an exception to this rule. If you go onto Medicare prior to age 65 due to a qualifying medical disability you may be able to enroll in a Medicare Supplement plan. Once you turn age 65 you will receive another open enrollment period that will allow you to get any Medicare Supplement plan without answering any health questions. Most folks who fall into this category do end up making a change to their current Medigap plan during their second open enrollment. Many times these folks may only be able to enroll in a Medicare Supplement Plan A when under the age of 65, but when they turn 65, they want to get better coverage and move to a Plan G.

Important Tip: Unless your state requires the Medicare Supplement insurance companies to offer at least one plan to folks on Medicare under the age of 65, you may not be able to take advantage of this first open enrollment window. The good news is that you could still enroll in a Medicare Advantage plan to limit your maximum out-of-pocket expenses.

Working Past Age 65

If you happen to decide you want to work past the age of 65, you can delay your enrollment into Part B of Medicare. Keep in mind, just as we discussed in Chapter 8 there are guidelines. The key thing to remember is that you must be covered under what meets the definition of 'credible coverage'. Most of the large employer group-based plans meet this definition.

For those folks who work for a small group employer, you will still need to sign up for Parts A & B as we discussed in Chapter 8. The big difference here is that if you decide to remain on the group plan you will miss out on your one-time Medicare Supplement open enrollment period. The good news is that there are certain provisions that will provide you with a guaranteed issue period. Keep in mind that the small group employer plan must still meet the definition of credible coverage.

Important Tip: If you are on a small group employer plan while working past age 65 you can still qualify for a guaranteed issue period that will allow you to purchase one of the following plans without medical underwriting: Medicare Supplement Plans A, B, D, G, K, or L. Once you decide to retire and you can show you have had credible coverage, you will receive a 63-day window which allows you to get any of the above mentioned Medigap plans without having to answer any health questions. The 63-day clock begins on the date your prior coverage ends.

CHAPTER 17: Avoiding the Confusing Landmines

Avoiding the Confusing Landmines

Medicare Television Ads

These are the television ads sponsored by Medicare and not the ones paid for by lead aggregators and call centers.

Every year many folks confuse the Medicare Annual Enrollment Period (AEP) with the one-time Medicare Supplement Open Enrollment Period. Trust me, with the way that Medicare phrases these commercials, it is easy to see why this happens.

I am sorry to say, that during the AEP you cannot change your Medicare Supplement plan without medical underwriting. Medicare calls the AEP an Open Enrollment Period. Once again, while they are calling it this, it does NOT apply to Medicare Supplements. The period that falls between October 15th and December 7th applies to Medicare Advantage and Part D prescription drug plans. During this period, you can do any of the following:

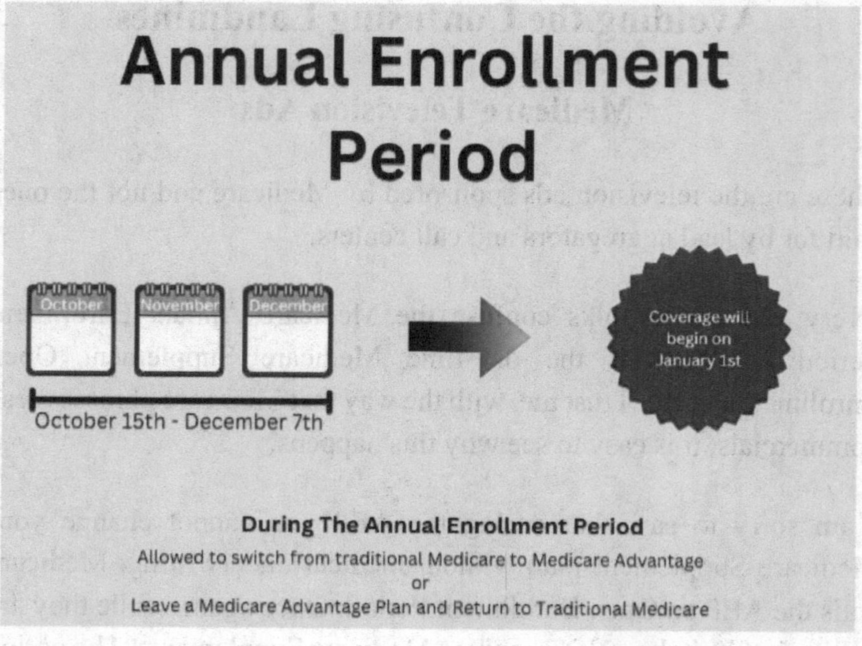

As you can see from the image above, Medicare Supplement plans are **not** included.

Why Your Doctor's Office Can Cause Even More Confusion

I have spent well over 30 years in the Medicare market. If you need a Medicare Supplement, Part D prescription drug plan or a Medicare Advantage plan, then I am someone you would call for advice. If you need a medical diagnosis, then you should call a doctor. It really is that simple.

Many times, folks will call their doctor's office and ask them what insurance plan they should get. Got any idea what companies their billing department is going to suggest? Whichever one is easiest for them to work with. They are not qualified to advise which plan would work best for you but typically will look for what reduces their workload. Can I blame them? Absolutely not! Does it mean you should take their advice? Absolutely not!!

Over the years, the most common complaint we here from clients is that they call their doctor's office and ask them if they participate with Medicare Supplement XYZ. The person answering the phone is going to typically look at a cheat sheet that is likely taped by their computer and if the company name is not on there, they will say they don't participate. Here is the problem. That list is not for Medicare Supplement plans but rather for Medicare Advantage plans that require the doctor's office to be part of a network. If the doctor is not in the network, then they don't participate with that plan.

Remember, a Medicare Supplement plan does **not** use a network. In fact, most claims fall under what is known as 'claims crossover' which is a fancy way of saying that the claim goes from the doctor's office to Medicare and then after Medicare pays it portion the claim is forwarded to the Medicare Supplement plan for it to pay its portion.

Another reason why your doctor's office is not a good place to get insurance advice from is that most really do not fully understand how all the different plans work, and which benefits you need. They can see how the plan covers the care you get at their office but will not understand how the plans work in other areas.

Important Tip: If you are considering a Medicare Advantage plan it will be much easier to simply allow one of our seasoned and well-educated advisors check the up-to-date carrier network database for all of your current physicians, hospitals, and other providers to see if they participate. This is especially important when you have past the mid-year point when a provider may opt to no longer participate within a plan's network.

Joe Namath and JJ Walker Don't Understand Medicare

Yes, we have all seen the commercials that seem to run 24 hours a day during the Annual Enrollment Period (October 15th-December 7th) where Joe Namath is telling you why you need to call the 800# on your screen to get all these extra benefits. Listen, Joe set some great records for the NY Jets back in his day like passing for 4,000+ yards in one season and completing over 1,800 passes during his career. I'm sorry to say that being inducted into the football hall of fame does not make him a Medicare expert.

I don't believe for a minute that Joe Namath believes he is anything other than a paid spokesperson, and that is all he should be viewed as. The same goes for JJ Walker who might very well be a funny comedian (depending on your tastes) and made millions of folks laugh when he was on television, but in all my years of being in the Medicare industry I have never heard a benefit being defined as 'Dyno-Mite'.

As I previously mentioned, these commercials walk a very fine line of being misleading. In fact, if you compare the current commercials to the ones just run a year ago you will see how much they have had to change the verbiage being used.

Why has this happened?

Well, let's look at just some of the statistics:

- 85% of the Medicare beneficiaries do not qualify for many of the extra benefits talked about due to their income being too high.
- According to CMS there was an increase in Medicare misleading marketing claims that rose from 15,500 complaints in 2020 to more than 39,000 in 2021.8

With misleading complaints more than doubling in just one year, I think that this speaks volumes as to why you do not want to get your Medicare guidance from these call centers.

CHAPTER 18: Conclusion You Made It

Congratulations…you made it to the end of the book! Yes, Medicare is boring and overwhelming, but now you have the basic knowledge needed to make a better decision. Do I recommend you run out and buy a new plan on your own? No, but now you can at least avoid some of the Medicare landmines that plenty of retiree's step on.

Senior Benefit Services, Inc.
ADDITIONAL ONLINE RESOURCES

Feel free to read our Medicare posts on www.seniorbenefitclient.com, take in a video or two at https://www.youtube.com/@seniorbenefitservices, or view up to date posts on our Facebook page https://www.facebook.com/SeniorBenefitServices/

The next step is to book your one-on-one call with one of our advisors, who will assess your individual needs and then guide you thru the 'Medicare Maze.' You can attend the call via phone or video chat, and the best news is that you don't need to have your checkbook handy. There is absolutely no cost or obligation for this service.

Q: How do you get paid?

A: There is no cost to you since we are paid directly by the insurance company. Whichever plan or company that works best for your personal situation will pay us directly at no cost to you.

Q: Do you only work with retirees who are turning 65?

A: Absolutely NOT! We work with all ages who are on Medicare. We help thousands of retirees each year find more affordable plans that fit their specific needs.

Q: What if the prescription drug plan that I need is one you do not currently work with?

A: We will still make sure you understand the plan benefits and will guide you on how to enroll directly with the plan provider. Most agents will not do this since they are not paid by any plan provider they are not currently representing. Our main focus is you getting the benefits you need. We know if you get the best service, you will refer your friends and family to us.

Q: What is the difference between your company and a call center?

A: Unlike a call center, you will work with your own dedicated advisor. Your advisor is going to focus first on educating you and finding out what your exact needs are. They are well versed in understanding all parts of Medicare and the coverages that would work best for you. In addition, call center agents are trying to get you to enroll in a plan as soon as you call in. We understand that this can be overwhelming, so we move at your speed. There is no pressure for you to enroll when speaking with us.

Q: After I enroll will I ever hear from my advisor again?

A: Unlike other firms we stay in touch with you during the year and even provide you with a complimentary annual review to make sure you are still in the best plan for your needs. In addition, if there ever is a claim issue or another problem that arises, your advisor is just a quick call away to help.

LOCAL

State Health Insurance Assistance Program
(877)839-2675
www.shiphelp.org

FEDERAL

Centers for Medicare and Medicaid Services
1-800-MEDICARE
TTY 1-877-486-2048
www.medicare.gov

Social Security Administration
(800)772-1213
TTY 1-800-325-0778
www.ssa.gov
www.ssa.gov/locator (to find a local office)

References

1. Sarah O'Brien, "You can't put money in a health savings account once you're on Medicare. A House bill to change that comes with tradeoffs" CNBC, May 19, 2022, https://www.cnbc.com/2022/05/19/you-cant-save-in-hsa-on-medicare-a-bill-to-change-that-has-tradeoffs.html

2. Jackie Stewart, Sandra Block, "You Can Appeal a Medicare Premium Surcharge" Kiplinger, June 10, 2021, https://www.kiplinger.com/retirement/medicare/602937/you-can-appeal-a-medicare-premium-surcharge

3. National Council on Aging, "Medicare art D Cost-Sharing Chart" https://www.ncoa.org/article/medicare-part-d-cost-sharing-chart

4. Stein, Chiplin, and Kertesz, Medicare Handbook, 2021 Edition, (11-11); "What is TrOOP or True Out-Of-Pocket Costs" Q1Group LLC, https://q1medicare.com/PartD-WhatIs-TheTrueOutOfPocketExpense.php; Your Guide to Medicare Prescription Drug Coverage, 48, 65-66.

5. National Council on Aging, "How Does Medicare Work with VA Benefits and TRICARE for Life?" January 10, 2023, https://ncoa.org/article/how-does-medicare-work-with-va-benefits-and-tricare-for-life

6. Meredith Freed, Jeannie Fuglesten Biniek, Anthony Damico Tricia Neuman, "Medicare Advantage in 2022: Premiums, Out-of-Pocket Limits, Cost Sharing,

Supplemental Benefits, Prior Authorization, and Star Ratings" August 25, 2022,
https://www.kff.org/medicare/issue-brief/medicare-advantage-in-2022-premiums-out-of-pocket-limits-cost-sharing-supplemental-benefits-prior-authorization-and-star-ratings/

7. "Guaranteed Issue Rights, Centers for Medicare & Medicaid Services, last accessed April 5, 2023, https://www.medicare.gov/supplements-other-insurance/when-can-i-buy-medigap/guaranteed-issue-rights

8. Mark Miller, "Medicare Open Enrollment: Don't Let Deceptive Advertising Lead To Costly Mistakes", October 11, 2022, https://www.morningstar.com/retirement/medicare-open-enrollment-dont-let-deceptive-advertising-lead-costly-mistakes

www.ingramcontent.com/pod-product-compliance
Lightning Source LLC
Chambersburg PA
CBHW012257240726
48656CB00007B/2429

9 798988 958017